WASH THE FEET OF
THE WORLD

—— WITH ——

Mother
Teresa

WASH THE FEET OF THE WORLD

—— WITH ——

Mother

Teresa

CHARLES RINGMA

PIÑON PRESS ®

OUR GUARANTEE TO YOU

We believe so strongly in the message of our books that we are making this quality guarantee to you. If for any reason you are disappointed with the content of this book, return the title page to us with your name and address and we will refund to you the list price of the book. To help us serve you better, please briefly describe why you were disappointed. Mail your refund request to: PiñonPress, P.O. Box 35002, Colorado Springs, CO 80935.

ISBN 1-57683-422-0

Cover or photo: Jacqui Hurst/CORBIS
Creative Team: Don Simpson, Darla Hightower, Arvid Wallen, Glynese Northam

Unless otherwise identified, all Scripture quotations in this publication are taken from the HOLY BIBLE: NEW INTERNATIONAL VERSION® (NIV®). Copyright © 1973, 1978, 1984 by International Bible Society. Used by permission of Zondervan Publishing House. All rights reserved.

Ringma, Charles.
  Wash the feet of the world with Mother Teresa / Charles Ringma.
    p. cm.
Includes bibliographical references.
  ISBN 1-57683-422-0
  1. Teresa, Mother, 1910- 2. Missionaries of Charity--Biography. I. Title.
BX4406.5.Z8R56 2004
271'.97--dc22

                                    2003022060

Printed in Canada

1 2 3 4 5 6 7 8 9 10/ 09 08 07 06 05 04

For
the leaders and members of
Grandview Calvary Baptist Church,
East Vancouver, Canada—
a community of celebration and
faith, and service to the poor.

Contents

Preface

MOTHER TERESA IS ONE OF THE MOST STRIKING ICONS of the twentieth century. This diminutive woman, great in spiritual stature, has won the respect of millions for her ministry to the poorest of the poor.

While her life of service is undoubtedly the reason for her popularity, there is much more to her life. She is also a person of deep devotion and prayer, and a woman of singular courage, wisdom, and faith.

In this spiritual reader, it is all the dimensions of Mother Teresa's life that we wish to engage. We want to hear the heartbeat of her love for God. We want to enter the mystery of her adoration of Christ. We want to understand her courage and strength. We want to draw near to the quiet places of her life of prayer. And we wish to engage the passion of her service to the poor. Spirituality is never the province of our prayer life alone. Nor is it focused only on our deeds of love for the neighbor. Spirituality encompasses the whole of a life lived in God's presence.

It is this double theme of turning our face toward God and our hand toward the neighbor in need that also constitutes the focus of the companion volumes in this series: *Dare to Journey with Henri Nouwen, Seize the Day with Dietrich Bonhoeffer, Resist the Powers with Jacques Ellul,* and *Let My*

People Go with Martin Luther King Jr.

I am grateful to NavPress for their commitment to this series and their concern to bring to readers a Christian spirituality that is rooted in theology, the reading of Scripture, and the practices of the spiritual disciplines, and that also engages our world in loving service.

This is a spirituality that knows the practice of solitude and the work of justice, the need for prayer and transformative action, and the joy of worship and the pain of identification with those in great need.

Charles Ringma
Regent College
Vancouver, BC, Canada

Introduction

THE HUMAN CONDITION IS NOT SIMPLY ABOUT LIVING, but also about living well. And living well is not only a matter of having adequate economic resources and meaningful relationships. These are important, but there is much more to living well.

This "much more" is what this meditational reader is all about. And this may come as an initial surprise. One might ask, what do the sayings of Mother Teresa, who gave her life in service to the poorest of the poor, have to do with the meaning and well-being of my life?

In one sense, she has nothing to do with your life or mine. She belonged to a religious order. She lived a celibate life. She was committed to a life of poverty. And that is a very different kind of lifestyle from the one that the majority of us lead.

Yet, in another sense, Mother Teresa may have much to do with our lives. While it may sound preposterous, she may know something about what it means to live well. Maybe she can help us discover what this "much more" is all about.

So what are we talking about when we speak about "living well"? Several important themes immediately spring to mind. One has to do with living with meaning and purpose. The other has to do with wholeness. And two other themes are pressingly relevant: the spiritual quest and the willingness to give oneself in love and service to others.

A more careful look at these themes reveals them to be dynamically interrelated. Meaning, spirituality, wholeness, and service all belong together.

Putting all of this in theological language, one might say that living well is to be loved by God, to overcome sin and alienation, to grow in Christlikeness, and to grow in love and service to the neighbor and the stranger.

Mother Teresa's life has much to teach us about all of this. She is a lover of God and a servant to humanity. She is a woman of faith and of deep compassion. She knows about prayer and costly service. But she also knows about the quest for meaning and purpose.

Thus this meditational reader takes Mother Teresa as an important guide. Each reflection is woven around one of her key thoughts. And while these are all marked by great simplicity, they reflect a profundity that brings us back to the words of Jesus and the visionary power of the gospel.

Along with my reflections on these key thoughts of Mother Teresa there are appropriate Scriptures and thoughts for further reflection and prayer.

I have two suggestions for using these readings. The first is to use these reflections as part of one's daily rhythm of prayer, solitude, and meditation. The other is that this book may be helpful for a time of special retreat in which the wisdom of Mother Teresa is one's companion.

Introducing
Mother Teresa

To some extent, it is rather strange introducing Mother Teresa. She is so well known. So many people know the basic contours of her story: how this Loreto nun serving in a school in Calcutta began living among and serving the poorest of the poor. This inauspicious beginning led to the formation of the fast growing order, the Missionaries of Charity.

After being catapulted into world prominence, particularly through the media work of Malcolm Muggeridge, Mother Teresa went on to win the Nobel Peace Prize. After that, her every daring move in challenging world leaders to adopt peace, her opening houses of ministry in countries resistant to Christian missions, her faithful persistence in serving the poorest of the poor, and her every health problem toward the end of her life were splashed on TV screens and newspapers across the world.

In those latter years before her death in 1997, Mother Teresa was the counter-icon to Princess Diana of the United Kingdom. The one was the woman of beauty from a world of privilege. Mother

Teresa, the diminutive one, wizened and craggy faced, was the woman of endless compassion. By her life and service she challenged the values of a world that, in its pursuit of progress, happiness, and productivity, had forgotten about the wretched of the earth.

There is little doubt that Mother Teresa was a "great soul" in the way that Mahatma Gandhi was such a person. Both responded to the massive problems of the world with a visionary power that brought others to join their cause.

Mother Teresa was also a great Roman Catholic. Her church will surely elevate her to sainthood. And she will take her place alongside the great women of faith in that religious tradition. Mother Teresa will find her rightful place alongside Teresa of Avila and certainly Therese of Lisieux, whose name she adopted at her profession to become a religious nun.

But more importantly, Mother Teresa was an exemplary Christian. In her life and ministry she demonstrated the great theme of the incarnation. She was not only deeply transformed by the Christ of the Gospels, but she was a follower of Christ, leading her to a life of service and witness to the poorest of the poor. Downward mobility, servanthood, simplicity, and sacrifice characterized Mother Teresa's life and work.

In the secondary reading material you can find several biographies on Mother Teresa and the brief chronology at the back of this book can give you some of the key high points in her life.

In further introducing Mother Teresa, let me draw your attention to some important themes.

First, Mother Teresa demonstrates the importance of Christian spirituality. She is a woman of the spiritual disciplines. She is a person who practiced prayer, meditation, solitude, reflection, the reading of Scripture, and participation in the Eucharist.

Secondly, Mother Teresa not only knew about God, she loved God. She not only knew the salvation of Christ, she gave her life to Christ as one would give oneself to one's lover. God for her was not a doctrinal idea but a living presence. And she implicitly trusted this God to care and provide for her and her ministry.

Thirdly, Mother Teresa, in the spirit of Saint Francis of Assisi, sought to live the Beatitudes — the gospel within the gospel. Thus her way in the world was one of blessing others, peacemaking, healing, caring. She saw herself as a mere pencil in God's hand.

Fourthly, this servant of God knew the importance of Christian community. She served the Roman Catholic Church, and she founded a religious order. She recognized that we are not called to do God's work on our own. We are called into fellowship with the Father, the Son, and the Holy Spirit, and we are called into the fellowship of brothers and sisters in Christ. Together, we worship the Living God, and together we serve in our wounded world.

Finally, Mother Teresa most clearly demonstrated that, as a Christian, one does not live simply for oneself. One lives for God, for the reign of God, and one lives in love and service to the neighbor and needy. This service to the neighbor may indeed be costly. It may involve giving one's all, one's whole life. For Mother Teresa this self-giving, for the sake of Christ, was a giving in joy, not as a dutiful burden.

There is much that could be added to these introductory remarks and there are many questions: Was Mother Teresa a product of the old pre-Vatican II church? What about her stand against modern contraception? What about her focus on charity rather than the work of justice? And what about her theological idea that by serving the poor we are actually serving the hidden suffering Christ in the face of the poor?

These and other questions will remain. But so will the power of her witness. And so will the power of her words.

It is to these words that we now turn.

So, Lord, we want to be attentive, we want to listen carefully and reflect prayerfully. Empower us to love and serve you in our world.

If you are humble, nothing will touch you, neither praise nor disgrace, because you know what you are.

—MOTHER TERESA

‡

Deep Roots

Being Grounded in the God of Life

Remain in me, and I will remain in you. No branch can bear fruit by itself; it must remain in the vine. Neither can you bear fruit unless you remain in me.

JOHN 15:4

Life is, first of all, not entirely about doing and giving. And contrary to the values of our culture, it is not only about productivity and success. Life is rooted in receiving. It is sustained because so much has been given to us.

This is also true of the life of faith, the life that we live through the empowerment of the Spirit. The God of grace comes to embrace us. To renew us. To awaken us from our spiritual slumber. To let light into the deep caverns of our existence.

And even a life of giving and receiving is rooted in receptivity. Mother Teresa comments, "The contemplative and apostolic fruitfulness of our way of life depends on our being rooted in Christ Jesus our Lord."[1]

Just as water continues to bubble to the surface

from subterranean wells no matter how inhospitable the landscape, so those who live and abide in God by the Spirit can extend bread to a hungry world.

Being rooted in Christ gives the whole of our life its particular contours. Belonging to Christ and being indwelt by his Spirit is not simply relevant for the religious dimensions of life. It shapes our very being. And as such, it molds the ethical stances that we take.

To be in Christ means that we live life in ways that resonate with the life of Christ. This means that we want to please God more than ourselves. It means that we want to be a healing rather than a fracturing presence in the world. It means that we want to walk the way of forgiveness rather than that of retaliation.

While being in Christ is the gift of God's grace, there is nothing automatic about growing in Christ. This calls for a life of surrender, obedience, and faithful service. Growing in Christ invites us to a life of prayer and of service to those society so easily overlooks.

*Reflection: Receptivity is the joyful posture
that fills empty hands.*

REFLECTION 2

God's Embrace

Entering into God's Welcome

> *For if, when we were God's enemies, we were rec-*
> *onciled to him through the death of his Son, how*
> *much more, having been reconciled, shall we be*
> *saved through his life!*
>
> ROMANS 5:10

People may well have reasons for regarding God as being distant, demanding, or even vindictive. Sometimes these reasons flow from being hurt by the difficulties of life. The expectation was that God could have prevented these things.

But the heart of the biblical story makes it clear that God is neither distant nor malevolent. God is the one who draws near and enters the fray of life. And God's grace and love is toward us, even though God does not always do what we wish.

Mother Teresa puts this most personally and intimately. She writes, "If you look at the cross, you will see his head lowered to kiss you. You will see his arms stretched out to embrace you. You will see his heart open to welcome you."[2]

This is the heart of the biblical story. No matter what our questions, pain, or anger, God reaches toward us with an embrace of welcome, the word of forgiveness, and the oil of healing.

The place to flee to is not the place of resentment, but the place of welcome. And in that welcome we receive God's kiss of life.

Sadly, in our Western world we see God not as the one who welcomes and heals us, but as the God who demands and who restricts our freedom. We see the life of faith as one of difficult obedience rather than one of joyful companionship.

At this point it is important to separate the story of Christianity and the story of God. The two are not always the same. There have been times where the church has emphasized law rather than God's offer of grace, where it has advocated narrow demand rather than the wideness of God's mercy.

God comes to us not with the pointing finger that condemns, but with the embrace of love that melts the hardest heart and soothes the fearful soul.

Reflection: Where is there a greater welcome than with the God who continues to reach out to us even when we won't listen?

Beautiful for God

Serving Others for God's Glory

> *Here is my servant, whom I uphold, my chosen*
> *one in whom I delight; I will put my Spirit on him*
> *and he will bring justice to the nations.*
>
> ISAIAH 42:1

Touched by God's transforming grace, we can hardly live to the beat of old tunes and former values. God renews us to live for his glory and the well-being of others.

In grateful response, it is appropriate for us to ask in what ways we may please God and be a blessing to others.

Mother Teresa asked this question and responded that she wished to "do something beautiful for God"[3] by serving the poorest of the poor. We too can seek to be beautiful for God and find our own particular ways to honor God and let his light shine into our world.

We cannot all be beautiful for God in the same way. Some wish to bring glory to God in their art, others in their teaching, and others in the work of justice.

So whether it is our role in the home, at school, in the marketplace, in our neighborhood, or in the nation, we can all find ways to reflect something of the grace and goodness of God to others.

Being beautiful for God has God as the major focus. It has God's glory in view and not our own success. We can be beautiful for God in the silence of adoration, the fervency of prayer, and the ecstasy of contemplation. But we can also be beautiful for God in the love and care we have for those in our families and in our circle of friends.

But an equally great challenge in our world so religiously cynical is to be beautiful for God in the public arenas of life: at work, in politics, in the arts, in the work of justice, and in service to the poor. In all the spheres of life we are called to demonstrate God's embrace, forgiveness, restitution, and healing.

Prayer: Lord, let my life shine for you.
Amen.

Humility

Blind to Our Generosity and Virtues

*But when you give to the needy, do not let your
left hand know what your right hand is doing.*
MATTHEW 6:3

The life of faith is a gift from God's generous
heart and hand. Faith is never the fruit of our
own virtues. As a result, we can never be proud
of our spirituality. We can only be thankful for all
that God has done and continues to do in
sustaining and empowering us.

Similarly, there is little point in trying to measure the progress and development we think we are
making in the journey of faith. The more we try
regularly to check our spiritual pulse, the more
self-preoccupied we become.

Mother Teresa is right when she counsels, "I
must not count the stages in the journey . . .
[God] would have me make. I must not desire a
clear perception of my advance along the road."[4]

The main reason why all such measurement
is futile is because in self-forgetfulness we are
most godlike, and in our weakness we are

strong in the grace of God.

Faith does not look to our own virtues and abilities, and much less to our own achievements. Instead, it looks to the God of surprises who blesses when we least expect it.

The desire to measure our spiritual progress frequently springs not from the wells of holiness but from the pitfalls of insecurity. We doubt God's love and generosity, and we are uncertain about our obedience and our responses for service, and so we compare ourselves with others. In doing this, we usually come off second best.

This is no way to walk the journey of faith. Rather, rejoicing in all that God has done for us in Christ, and comforted and empowered by the Spirit, we can live in great generosity and kindness toward others, showing them the grace that God has so freely extended toward us.

> *Prayer: May my gaze ever be on who you*
> *are, oh my God, and not upon what I may*
> *do for you.*

With Great Love

The Heartbeat of Our Doing

If I give all I possess to the poor and surrender my body to the flames, but have not love, I gain nothing.

1 CORINTHIANS 13:3

Many contemporary Christians know a lot about a busy activism. We try to do a lot for God and others. And while this is most appropriate, the source of life and our sense of identity and well-being does not lie in our much-doing.

The secret of life lies elsewhere. It lies in being loved by God and others, and it is expressed in deeds born out of love.

Mother Teresa has expressed this most clearly: "What matters is not how much we do, but how much love we put in what we do."[5] Here she echoes the heartbeat of the gospel, which identifies love as the greatest gift we receive and which we may give to others.

Our service can come out of duty or our own needs and compulsions. It can also spring from guilt or inappropriate use of power. But the gospel invites us to drink from the spring of God's love for us in Christ and empowers us to carry this into all we do.

People do not always first need things. They need to be known, welcomed, loved, and then served in appropriate ways. Therefore, the gift that we may give to others is not the gift of our busyness or our frenetic service, but the gift of our self-giving, time, and hospitality.

Being present to the other, even to the other whom we would normally bypass, challenges so many of our assumptions and calls us to a deeper conversion. For while we may wish to do that which we think is productive and significant, God may well call us to serve the least and the marginalized.

These perspectives are equally relevant for the home and for our friends. There too, the great gift is not, first of all, things, but the gift of love and availability.

Reflection: The greatest gift is to love the other unreservedly.

REFLECTION 6

A Second Call

God's Ongoing Work of Transformation

> *Brothers, choose seven men from among you who are known to be full of the Spirit and wisdom. We will turn this responsibility over to them.*
>
> ACTS 6:3

The most important and basic call we will ever receive from God is the call to embrace God's love and forgiveness and to become a part of God's kingdom purposes. All subsequent calls have to do with serving God in particular ways and places.

Mother Teresa first joined the Loreto nuns. Much later she was called to serve the poorest of the poor in Calcutta, which led to the founding of the Missionaries of Charity. Of this she says, "It was a call within my vocation. It was a second calling."[6]

All the followers of Jesus receive various callings beyond the primary call to faith in Christ and becoming part of the community of faith. For some this may lead to becoming an overseas missionary. But for others the callings of God have to do with a life of witness and service in the family, the workplace, and the neighborhood.

None of these callings is more important than the others. But what is important is that all require faith and faithfulness. All must be accompanied by prayer. All must spring out of love. All must seek to glorify God. All must seek to bless those they serve.

While Mother Teresa stresses the importance of the call to serve the poorest of the poor, she is equally adamant that we are to serve those within our family.

The sphere of service is not the most relevant matter, for we are called to be light and salt wherever we find ourselves, and this does include the world of economics and politics. But the more fundamental issue is the way in which we serve.

Do we serve to bless the other? Do we love in order to free the other? Do we give in order to empower the other? And do we do all of these things in order to bring glory to the God who has so freely blessed us in Christ?

Prayer: Lord, make me ever open to the leading of your Spirit. Amen.

REFLECTION 7

Silence

The Road to Greater Attentiveness

*Be still, and know that I am God; I will be
exalted among the nations, I will be
exalted in the
earth.*

PSALM 46:10

It is not only that we live in a world full of words
and images that ever seek to grab our interest
and attention where silence remains a scarce
commodity for us. It is also that it is difficult to
stop our inner talking even when all is quiet
around us.

Moreover, so much of our external and internal busyness is carried over into our relationship
with God. We are busy with God in our praying
and planning. We know little of silence with God.

Mother Teresa reminds us that "God is a friend
of silence—we need to listen to God because it's
not what we say but what he says to us and
through us that matters."[7]

To hear God we need to learn the art of internal silence. It's the practice of the seeking heart and
the yearning spirit.

This seeking springs from an openness that recognizes that it's more important for us to hear from God than it is for us to speak to God. What we receive in this pregnant silence can become the fruit of our service to others.

So how do we come to this pregnant silence when so much in our world and lives militate against it?

There are clearly no strategies and certainly no easy answers. But there are some important dimensions. The first is the basic recognition that God is God and we are not. Therefore, we have to grow in trust and in humility before God. God will act. It is not for us to be forever planning and strategizing. We also have to learn to wait and be still.

Secondly, internal silence is the gift of God's Spirit. When we become aware of the Spirit's work in gaining our attention, we may fall silent to hear his words of direction and encouragement.

Meditation: To be still is to be receptive to the still, small voice of the Spirit.

REFLECTION 8

Prayer

The Joy of Communion

By day the LORD directs his love, at night his song is with me—a prayer to the God of my life.
PSALM 42:8

Mother Teresa reminds us that "prayer is the food of the spiritual life."[8] And just as we should not eat an unbalanced diet, so our praying should not be reduced to fast-food eating habits.

This is not at all to suggest that we can't send quick and short prayers upward to God when we need help. The God of heaven and earth is open even to our whispers and whimpers. But as the psalmist suggests, prayer is also a life of communion with God. It is living in God's presence, surrounded by his love. And this evokes within us the song of hope and gratitude. As a result, the theme of thank you, Lord, becomes our heartbeat. And praise floats, not only from our lips, but reverberates in our very being.

In communion, our life is sustained and enriched. In the relationship between the Great Lover and the beloved, life is imparted that fuels us for the journey whether the path is smooth or rough.

It is important that we remind ourselves that prayer is not to take place only at the genesis or the conclusion of a project or in a phase of our life's journey. Sadly, this often occurs. We pray fervently at the beginning of something—Lord help us, direct us, and bless us.

At the conclusion of something we must also remember to give our thanks. But the whole project and the whole journey need to be bathed in prayer. Here we often fail. We become self-confident or lazy and prayer disappears from the most important part of the project or journey—the middle. Prayer for the middle is what lays the foundation for a good conclusion.

Thought: Prayer is not the luxury of the saint, but the bread of all who travel faith's pathway.

Incarnate

An Embodiment of God's Good News

> *But we have this treasure in jars of clay to show that this all-surpassing power is from God and not from us.*
>
> 2 Corinthians 4:7

God's good news has come to us not in words but in a person, Jesus Christ. And while we are thankful for the written Word, we worship the Living Word who came among us to show us the love and grace of the heavenly Father.

In a similar way, we are invited not only to speak God's good news to people, but to be good news as well. In this we recognize that in our service, word and deed must go together. We can't speak of forgiveness without being forgiving and we can't speak of love without demonstrating a love that serves the other.

Mother Teresa testifies, "The word of God has come to you and has become flesh in you."[9] While she may have primarily had her sisters in view, this statement challenges all of us. The words of the gospel need to nestle in our hearts and weave their way into the fabric of our lives so that we live the gospel.

There is nothing easy about this. We can only be the gospel to others by God's grace and enabling. To share the gospel and to embody the gospel mean that we have to find ways to connect with people so that we have the opportunity to do God's good to them.

This means that we have to learn to draw close, to befriend, to listen well, and to serve in ways that bless and empower others. This is usually a big challenge for us, for we are often much too busy to see the needs of others. And even when we do, we are usually quick with trite answers and fast solutions.

But to be God's good news to others also involves reflecting the patience of God, the willingness to journey with others and even to suffer with them.

Prayer: Lord, may your words of life find a home in my heart. And may my hands bring your bread and wine to a seeking world. Amen.

Possessions

Their Benefits and Their Temptations

*Give me neither poverty nor riches, but give me
only my daily bread.*

PROVERBS 30:8

There is no suggestion in the biblical story that
one should not be creative, work well, and
enjoy the fruits of one's labor. Being creative
reflects our being made in God's image. And
working well expresses the call to care for and
shape the earth and to be a blessing to the human
community.

But the biblical story does not advocate that we
simply live for ourselves. And it warns us that the
desire for possessions and much-having can con-
sume our lives.

Mother Teresa reminds us that "the more you
possess, the more you are preoccupied; the less you
possess, the freer you are."[10] The latter motif is true
of her order, the Missionaries of Charity. Can it also
be true of us?

I believe it can be true in several ways. In sharing
from our resources, we break the seductive hold

of possessions over our lives. And in simplifying our lives, we open spaces for prayer and service.

When possessions are received as God's good gifts and when they are shared with those in need, possessions are not a problem, but a welcome resource. But having this welcome resource brings not only blessings, but also great responsibility. To be good stewards of what we have is always a great challenge, for we so easily assume that what we have is ours to do with as we please.

We constantly need to be reminded that things are not simply ours, even though legally they may be. Morally and ethically we are called by the gospel to use our resources not only for our family and friends but also for the kingdom of God and for the neighbor in need. Thus the right use of possessions will always call us to a deeper conversion.

*Prayer: Lord, thank you for the gifts that come from your good hand. May my hand be open to others as your hand is open to me.
Amen.*

Self-Forgetting

Embracing the Quest for a True Identity

> *If anyone would come after me, he must deny*
> *himself and take up his cross and follow me.*
> MARK 8:34

Our contemporary culture emphasizes the importance of self-development and self-assertion. We have to make of life what we can, and we do this by grasping and striving.

This perspective fails to see that so much of life is not what we do but what has been given and what we have joyfully received. It also fails to see that we gain not simply by taking but by giving.

Self-giving is intrinsic to a healthy rhythm of life. Mother Teresa reminds us that "by forgetting yourself you find yourself."[11]

By self-forgetting we do not mean self-negation. This is not the doubtful art of putting oneself down. This is not the practice of a sense of inferiority. It is precisely the opposite. It is out of a sense of being loved by God and of having received so much, that we can bend our heart, ear, and hand to the other who is in need. And in reaching out and serving the other we grow into the persons God desires us to be.

This touches one of the great mysteries of human existence and exposes the lie of Western materialism and self-preoccupation. In the West, we have this idea that happiness is gained when we look after ourselves. And the more we can focus on ourselves, the better off we will be.

But the gospel has a very different vision of life based on the self-giving of Christ for our salvation, healing, and renewal. Christ gave of himself in order to bless humanity. And we, who have been marked by his grace and Spirit, are similarly called to give of ourselves to bless others. In doing this, we are also blessed.

Meditation: I can never become the person that God intends through a self-protecting isolation, but only in relationships where I receive and give.

REFLECTION 12

For God Alone

Living for God's Purposes

*Jesus gave them this answer: "I tell you the truth,
the Son can do nothing by himself; he can do only
what he sees his Father doing, because whatever
the Father does the Son also does."*

JOHN 5:19

Jesus lived to bring glory to his Father in
heaven.

Mother Teresa lived to bring glory to God in her
service to the poorest of the poor. And in that she
gave of herself. She gave her all.

She counsels us also to be radical in our love
and devotion to God. "All that you have and all
that you are," she exclaims, "let it be for Him and
Him alone."[12]

This challenge is difficult for us. Our culture
encourages us to live for ourselves. It knows little
of living radically for others. And yet, we need to
grow into this new way of being. Christ gave his
life for us and in his grace claims us for himself.
To live for God, therefore, is but a response to his
love and grace. And to give our all, as he gave his

life, is to pattern our life on the life of Christ.

Living for God and giving God our all does not mean that we have to become pious by withdrawing from the world and its concerns. To wholly love God does not mean that we despise or neglect his creation. The opposite is true. To wholly love God involves loving all that is God's concern.

And so we love God in acts of worship, prayer, and adoration, and in the practice of solitude and silence. We also love God in serving those within our immediate responsibility. But love of God also finds its expression in love of neighbors and work colleagues and in care for the created order.

All that God loves we are to love for his glory and honor.

Reflection: To live for God's glory is to live a life of obedience empowered by God's grace.

The Gift of Joy

A Welcome Surprise in
Times of Difficulty

*You turned my wailing into dancing; you removed
my sackcloth and clothed me with joy.*

PSALM 30:11

Our culture constantly echoes the idea that we
have a right to be happy and that real happiness lies in the possession of the many things that
society claims enhance our status. These things are
mainly consumer products. That this is sheer myth
is evidenced by the general unhappiness that particularly characterizes societies of the First World.

That happiness needs far deeper sources is
almost self-evident. Happiness is present when we
are safe, have good relationships, and are blessed
in particular ways, not only because we have
material resources.

While joy is a close cousin to happiness, it is
also significantly different. Joy is a surprising gift
that is not dependent on our circumstances.
Mother Teresa notes that "we are truly humble . . .
when we have joy in the hour of humiliation."[13]

In the places of pain and difficulty, joy can visit us and well up within us, because we know that God is also there working his mysterious purposes in us. Joy reminds us that the difficulties of the present are not the whole story. Joy suggests that in good and bad times, we are in God's care and love.

Thus, while our culture constantly promises happiness, the gospel offers us joy. And the source of this joy is not the possession of many things, but to be loved and nurtured by the God of all grace. Joy comes when God smiles upon us. It comes when grace abounds. It wells up when forgiveness is extended. It comes when God meets us in the place of prayer and solitude. And even in the darkest places when all seems lost, the God who gives joy longs to be our companion.

Thought: Joy is the gateway of hope.

The Whole Christ

Bringing the Whole Gospel to a Broken World

And I pray that you, being rooted and established in love, may have power, together with all the saints, to grasp how wide and long and high and deep is the love of Christ.

EPHESIANS 3:17-18

We are invited in the biblical story to embrace the offer of new life in Christ. But we are also invited to grow in Christ. And this means becoming more and more like him.

This growth may happen in many ways. Our time of friendship in prayer deepens the relationship. Our participation in the teaching and sacramental life of the community of faith consolidates our faith. And participating in serving others in the name of Christ grows us into greater conformity to the Master, who came not to be served but to save and give his life as a ransom for humanity. It is out of being shaped by Christ that our service to others and our proclamation of the good news are to flow.

Mother Teresa challenges us to not give "people a broken Christ, a lame Christ, a crooked Christ deformed by you."[14] In other words, let us not attempt to bring a gospel only by words. Instead, let us bring the good news in love, words, and deeds out of the joy of what God has done in our own lives.

To bring the whole Christ to the whole world remains a big challenge for us. Not only are our churches still deeply divided, but our vision to serve the poor in out-of-the-way places is often dim or nonexistent.

All of this is not to say that we must be perfect before we can bring the whole Christ to the world. For finally, like John the Baptist, we have to point away from ourselves and point to him—the Lamb of God who takes away the sin of the world. We are always challenged not only to preach this gospel, but to live it and to serve as Christ served.

Prayer: Lord, may my life ever be open to all that you are seeking to do in me. And out of your goodness and love empower me to be your witness and servant. Amen.

REFLECTION 15

Prayer's Secret

Enlarging Our Receptivity

> *How lovely is your dwelling place, O LORD*
> *Almighty! My soul yearns, even faints, for the*
> *courts of the LORD; my heart and my flesh cry out*
> *for the living God.*
>
> PSALM 84:1-2

Prayer is the language of the heart. As such, it carries many secrets and is shrouded in mystery. We don't understand all that prayer can do and all that it may accomplish.

Prayer is to the practice of spirituality what wheat is to bread making. It is basic and fundamental. In fact, spirituality would cease to be if prayer became a total stranger.

So prayer is the friend. It is intrinsic to the life of faith. And Mother Teresa suggests that "prayer enlarges the heart until it is capable of containing God's gift of himself."[15]

Thus prayer's most basic orientation is not to gain things that we think we need, but to gain God and to enjoy him more fully. In this way, we are enriched in ways that will always surprise us.

Prayer opens the heart to God in love, friendship, and surrender. And in this openness we receive more than we could ever expect.

All of this is not to suggest that it is only in prayer that our capacity for God grows. God uses many ways to shape our lives into greater conformity to his will and purpose. In worship, through teaching, in the blessing of fellowship, in the grace of the sacraments, and in loving service our hearts are enlarged to receive God more fully. But we also grow in the difficult places. In the dark night of the soul, in times of seeming barrenness, in the places of brokenness and emptiness, and in times of suffering our hearts are enlarged so that we may more fully live the mystery of God.

Thought: Prayer is friendship with God.

Kept in God's Love

Living Out of Life's Greatest Gift

Yet the LORD set his affection on your forefathers and loved them.

DEUTERONOMY 10:15

The greatest thing that can ever happen to us is not that we fall in love with someone, but that we are loved. And the Greatest Lover is not mother or friend, but the God of the universe.

To be loved by God is sheer miracle and undeserved grace. That God should love me and make himself known to me is almost unbelievable. But the biblical story is full of these surprises.

Our love for God is a response to God's love for us. And it is within this frame that Mother Teresa's observation is correct: "We can only find true happiness and peace when we are in love with God."[16]

To love God is to order our whole life toward him in worship, obedience, and service. And while this may sound arduous, it is in fact the opposite. To be loved by God and to love this Great Lover gives life a fundamental substructure that the challenges and difficulties of life cannot subvert. In fact, no greater security and blessedness can come our way. This movement of love becomes the central reality of our whole existence.

However, to live in God's love does not mean that nothing difficult will come our way. God's love for us does not guarantee a smooth ride in the journey of life. In fact, we may have to go through many difficulties and trials.

But God's love does mean that God will journey with us, that there will be grace for the difficult times, and that good does come to those who trust in the Lord. This good, however, is not always the good that we might expect, but it is the good that God gives.

Prayer: Lord, your love makes me whole. May my feeble love honor you. Amen.

REFLECTION 17

Inner Life

The Practice of Prayer and Solitude

*Very early in the morning, while it was still
dark, Jesus got up, left the house and went off to
a solitary place, where he prayed.*

MARK 1:35

One might have thought that Jesus, Son of God
and Son of Man, could have quite easily been
busy with his ministry and that he did not need
time for prayer and reflection. That this was not
the case should be a powerful signal to us who
claim to be his followers.

Mother Teresa speaks of the need for "an
intense inner life."[17] By this she does not mean a
self-preoccupied introspection. Nor is she
promoting psychological and archaeological
expeditions of the inner person.

The inner life she is referring to is one of adoration, solitude, listening, and prayer. It has to do
with becoming attentive to God. It is the art of
receptivity and the act of abandonment. And these
are the things we moderns are not good at. Our
culture and our churches demand a continual

activism. And while we are called to witness and service, we are also called to friendship with God.

Taking time to be still in God's presence is not wasted time. It is, instead, the time for renewal and hearing.

The contemporary Western church is well-known for its activism and social concern. But there is a dearth of saintliness and godliness. Clearly something is missing and Mother Teresa may well be pointing us in the right direction.

The cultivation of the inner life through the exercise of the Christian spiritual disciplines, of which prayer is just one, is not an optional extra in the Christian life. It is basic and essential, for it deepens our relationship with God and empowers us for service.

Prayer does not first of all change others; it changes us.

Thought: *What we nurture in the inner life will become the fruit of our activism.*

Strength in Weakness

Learning to Rely Wholly on God

We always carry around in our body the death of Jesus, so that the life of Jesus may also be revealed in our body.

2 CORINTHIANS 4:10

Central to the heart of the biblical story is the Paschal mystery. Out of Christ's death, new life comes.

When we embrace the gospel—that Christ died and rose again that we might live by the grace and power of God—we experience this Paschal mystery. Spiritually dead apart from God, we are now alive in God through the Spirit.

This death-resurrection motif lies at the heart of the Christian journey of faith as well. There are things we must continue to die to, in order that God's new life may grow in us.

This must also occur in the area of service to others. We are often so self-assured and self-sufficient in helping others. But Mother Teresa points us in another direction. She notes, "Sometimes I feel so helpless and weak. I think that is why God uses me."[18]

While God wishes to use our talents, gifts, and resources, God cannot use our self-sufficiency. Just as we need to learn to live by the grace of God, so we need to learn to serve others in humility and in God's gentle strength.

This posture of humility never means that we belittle ourselves. It has nothing to do with the false humility that is self-negating and self-critical. It is quite the opposite. It is loving God with all our soul, mind, and strength, and loving others with conviction and great generosity.

But it also comes from the recognition that finally all is from God and not from ourselves. Our strength and our humility are all gifts from the God who has given us all things.

Reflection: God can make better use of our weakness than our strength.

Mere Creatures

Acknowledging That God Alone Is God

> *Though the LORD is on high, he looks upon the
> lowly, but the proud he knows from afar.*
> PSALM 138:6

There are two themes that continue to echo in Western culture. The one, the theme of self-sufficiency, suggests that we don't really need God. We can manage life and society by ourselves. With our abilities and our technologies, we can make life purposeful and secure.

The other theme, closely related, is that of the messianic complex that characterizes the West. We have the best and this is what others need. And so we will give the rest of the world the good things that we believe they so rightly should have.

These cultural distortions, which also characterize our personal lives, indicate that our understanding of who God is and who we are is badly out of focus. God is relegated to the sidelines and it is we who have become all powerful and significant.

But Mother Teresa reminds us that "the saints . . .

have been able to see God and to see themselves and have noted the difference."[19] In other words, they have been able to acknowledge that God alone is God and we are not.

To live this way has many implications. It means that prayer is a part of one's life. It also means that one is characterized by humility. Furthermore, one becomes focused on doing what God wants in our world rather than doing our own thing.

To acknowledge our creatureliness is a good thing. It invites us to be realistic. We cannot do everything and everything does not finally depend on us.

But in acknowledging who we are, we are called to confess who God is. The God who is greater than us. The God who made all things and sustains all things by the might of his power.

This God is also the God of grace in whose goodness we can live and by whose power we can serve.

Thought: Pleasing and obeying God is the right focus of our lives.

Contemplation

A Spirituality of Love of God and Neighbor

*Love and faithfulness meet together; righteous-
ness and peace kiss each other. Faithfulness
springs forth from the earth, and righteousness
looks down from heaven.*

PSALM 85:10-11

To be a contemplative does not mean that one
must live in a monastery. We are all invited to
be contemplatives no matter what our calling and
profession may be.

And to be a contemplative is more than being
a reflective person. It is more than being a person
of prayer and solitude. The heart of the contemplative experience is to see God. It is the experience
of God's presence. It is seeing God in all of life.

Mother Teresa claims that the members of her
order are "contemplatives in the heart of the
world."[20] They seek God's face in the place of
prayer, the Eucharist, and the life of Christian community. They also seek God's presence in their
service to the poor.

We are all invited to seek God in prayer and in stillness, but also in our families, our places of work, and our neighborhoods. We seek God, but we believe that he is already among us by his Spirit. But the contemplative person seeks to be attentive to God's loving grace and care among us and to see God more fully.

To be a contemplative does not mean that one is impractical or so heavenly minded to be no earthly good. The opposite is in fact the case, even though we have the idea that contemplatives are far removed from life. The contemplative experience is all about God. It is seeing God with the eyes of faith in birth and in dying, in family and in work, in church and in society, in prayer and in economics.

This is not mere wishful thinking, but believing that God the Creator and Redeemer chooses to presence himself in every nook and corner of life.

Reflection: The contemplative has
the eyes of faith.

The Gift of Time

Living Meaningfully for the Greater Good

> *For there is a proper time and procedure for every matter, though a man's misery weighs heavily upon him.*
>
> ECCLESIASTES 8:6

Most of us see time as a commodity of which we never have enough. And so we complain that we do not have enough time for this or that.

This is particularly a problem when we always seek to want and do more. Pulled by the pressures to achieve and to have more, we are ever scrambling from one activity to another. In the work of Christian service and especially in seeking to serve the poor, where the need is so great and our resources are so few, there is ever the temptation to do more.

But Mother Teresa's counsel is wise and insightful: "Take time to think . . . to pray . . . to laugh."[21] For these are not simply the welcome breaks from our own busy service, but the fuel to sustain our very being.

Our much-doing so quickly frames our horizon and defines our being. But this is having things back to front. Love, joy, relationship, and contemplation should define who we are, and serving others is the overflow of love.

In all of this, it is important for us to acknowledge the slow work of God. While we are in a hurry to do the work of God, we fail to realize that God works differently. In God's time, his purposes are fulfilled. And for us this often seems to be so awfully slow.

But like the farmer who works hard at sowing and equally hard at reaping patiently waits for the crop to grow and mature, so we too need to understand God's rhythm of work and sabbath, service and laughter, engagement and reflection.

Thought: If we have time to think and pray, we have time to be creative and renewed.

REFLECTION 22

Presence

Journeying with Others

> *For Christ's love compels us, because we are con-*
> *vinced that one died for all, and therefore all died.*
> *And he died for all, that those who live should no*
> *longer live for themselves but for him who died*
> *for them and was raised again.*
>
> 2 CORINTHIANS 5:14-15

The gift of God's transforming grace is one that liberates us from sin's domination and frees us for love and service. And in serving others the greatest blessing we can bring is often not the giving of things, but the gift of ourselves.

Mother Teresa underscores this in her words to her sisters, "Do not look for spectacular works. What is important is the gift of ourselves."[22]

This may initially sound surprising. Don't the poor need food, housing, and healthcare? Should we, therefore, not give them what they most basically need? The answer is, of course, we should give as much as we can. But others can't be the recipients of only our welfare and generosity. They are people who need to be loved and known. They welcome our interest and friendship, not simply our giving. Journeying with others through the highs and lows of their daily realities is the great gift we can give. And this giving of ourselves is possible because God has so freely given his grace to us.

To journey with people, rather than simply to give them things, has important implications. The most important of these is that we are invited to be an incarnational presence to the poor. What this means is that we must be willing to become "poor" ourselves. This involves a deep conversion for those who come from the Western world where much-having, abundance, and acquisition are so much a part of people's lifestyle. For to be an incarnational presence among the poor will surely mean the embrace of downward mobility and living a life of relinquishment.

Reflection: While we may always want to do more, we should not withhold the greater gifts—the gifts of companionship and solidarity.

In Christ

Living in His Grace and Care

I keep asking that the God of our Lord Jesus Christ, the glorious Father, may give you the Spirit of wisdom and revelation, so that you may know him better.

EPHESIANS 1:17

There are many values that we can live by. In our pluralistic societies, the options for differing kinds of lifestyles are becoming more numerous. It seems that the Christian way of life is presently not a hot favorite. People are not enamored with Christianity or with the church.

But to live Jesus' way will always be a powerful attraction and challenge. In Jesus we see what God is like. And in him we find salvation and transformation. And it is Jesus who calls us to walk the way of forgiveness and peace. He calls us to serve others and to love our enemies.

Mother Teresa counsels us to "put yourself completely under the influence of Jesus."²³ This means not only that we should imitate Jesus, but also that Jesus should live within us by the Spirit to motivate and empower us. The good news is not only that Christ died for our sins, but that he rose again to live within us.

To be under the influence of Jesus is never primarily an outward constraint, but an inner motivation. Here I am referring to the great mystery of faith—that Christ lives within us by the power of the Holy Spirit, who is God's gift to us.

It is the Spirit within us who makes us hunger after righteousness and seek God's kingdom. It is the Spirit who works in us the virtues of Christ. And it is the Spirit who empowers us for Christian service.

Thus, to be under the influence of Christ means that we are called to live in and by the Holy Spirit, who constantly births the life of Jesus within us.

Prayer: Lord Jesus, so fill me with your
presence that I may live in your ways.
Amen.

Contemplation

The Adoration of Christ

*And we, who with unveiled faces all reflect the
Lord's glory, are being transformed into his likeness with ever-increasing glory, which comes
from the Lord, who is the Spirit.*

2 CORINTHIANS 3:18

While we may have words to describe the
way in which God embraces us and the
way in which we relate to God, it is finally a mystery. God is with us and we are invited to live in
God's presence.

To live in this way means that we need to be
attentive to God, even as God cares for us and sustains us. This attentiveness has to do with
discerning God's way with us and being sensitive
to the movement of God's Spirit within our lives.

Attentiveness can also be a discipline that we
cultivate. Mother Teresa speaks of this. She
notes, "Often a deep and fervent look at Christ
is the best prayer; I look at him and he looks at
me."[24] The contemplation of Christ is being
attentive to his words, Spirit, and presence. It has

the posture of openness. It is a careful listening. It involves worship and adoration.

And what is the purpose of all this? It is an acknowledgment of who Christ is and what he has done for us. And it is becoming like him, conformed to his ways and his example of love and service.

The contemplation of Christ is never only a contemplation of the victorious Christ. It is also a contemplation of the suffering Christ. The importance of this cannot be overemphasized. If we only look to the victorious Christ, then we have no message of consolation for those who are walking the difficult road of faith. And if we only see the suffering Christ, then we have no message of empowerment and transformation.

Being attentive to Christ is to see him as prophet, priest, and king. It is seeing him as the Bethlehem babe and the triumphant Lord. It is acknowledging him as suffering servant and Lord of all.

Prayer: In looking upon you, oh Christ, may I see myself more truly in my need and you more fully in your grace. Amen.

Evangelical Poverty

Relinquishment and Piety

> [We] should live as . . . those who use the things
> of the world, as if not engrossed in them. For this
> world in its present form is passing away.
>
> 1 CORINTHIANS 7:29,31

We are invited to grow into God so that we become possessed by him. This is never a possession of oppression and exploitation, but one of freedom and enhancement.

If we are not possessed by God, then other things may well possess us. And in our contemporary world, the endless quest for much-having can become an oppressive power in our lives.

Mother Teresa invites us into a spirituality of relinquishment. She comments, "Poverty is freedom . . . so that what I possess doesn't own me . . . so that my possessions don't keep me from sharing or giving of myself."[25]

This ability to live openhandedly with what we have is a great grace. It is a grace that frees us for the service of God in the service of others. In resisting the powers of our age, we are invited to a downward mobility. Instead of always wanting more, we live with open hearts and open hands toward those we may bless in Christ's name.

To speak of poverty as a freedom does need to be carefully nuanced. For the poor, poverty is not a freedom. It is an oppression. Many poor are the exploited ones of the earth. They live each day with the heavy burden of survival.

But for those who have much, poverty can be a freedom. Here we mean a poverty of spirit that leads to serving the poor through acts of generosity.

In the true following of God we will always have our hearts turned toward the poor, for God carries them in his heart and seeks for us to become his hands.

Reflection: Evangelical poverty is embracing downward mobility for the sake of the gospel.

Reflection 26

The Little

*Acting in a World So
Overwhelmingly Unjust*

*Seek good, not evil, that you may live. Then the
Lord God Almighty will be with you, just as you
say he is.*

Amos 5:14

Our contemporary culture so emphasizes bigness and success that this has filtered even into
our thinking about Christian ministry. As a result,
some Christians are afraid to attempt anything in
the form of new strategies of care and service to
others unless they are guaranteed success.

Yet, so much of what we do cannot be thought
about in such terms. In doing the deeds of love and
care in the home, the workplace, or the neighborhood, we are simply adding a little goodness
to the often bitter taste of life.

Mother Teresa, whose mission organization has
spread across the world, is nevertheless bluntly
realistic. She states, "What we do is less than a drop
in the ocean."[26]

This perspective invites us to take small steps

in the slow march of God. We are encouraged to do the doable. We are challenged to be daring in responding in small ways, even though so much remains to be done. We are invited to be practical, even when the needs far outweigh our resources and faith.

Some people are only mobilized into action when the project is big and significant. Others are not mobilized at all because the problems of a neighborhood, people group, or nation are totally overwhelming.

Between these two polarities lie various mediating approaches. And the most basic is to respond to the call of God in doing something about what lies immediately in front of us. Human need usually does not need to be sought in faraway places.

A willingness to help one person may become a steppingstone to the formation of a ministry that blesses many.

> *Thought: The little is never little for the one or two who are helped and blessed.*

Practicality

Bringing Hands to Heart and Mind

What good is it, my brothers, if a man claims to have faith but has no deeds? Can such faith save him?

JAMES 2:14

Although the heart of Christianity has to do with the good news of what God has done in Christ for our salvation and transformation, this does not mean that Christianity is only about words. Rather, the Christian faith is concerned with words and deeds.

Throughout the biblical story we see not only a God who speaks words of love and hope, but also a God who acts in history to set his people free. And in the ministry of Jesus we learn of the mysteries of the kingdom of God as well as Christ's acts of power bringing healing and deliverance.

Words and deeds belong together. And from the ministry of Mother Teresa we learn of the importance of the most practical of deeds in the service of Christ. She comments, "I rolled up my sleeves immediately, rearranged the whole room, found water and a broom, and began to sweep the floor."[27]

Christ was the Word made flesh. The Eucharist is food and drink. And love does not simply speak the words of kindness. It also performs the deeds of care and practical service.

The deeds of service that the gospel calls us to are not restricted to certain areas of life. It is not simply deeds of love for our family or friends, but also service to the neighbor and stranger.

Wherever we find ourselves, in the home, the neighborhood, the church, or the workplace, we are invited to be the servants of Christ by blessing others. But in the midst of all of that, the gospel also reminds us to remember especially the poor. In serving them, we most clearly demonstrate that the kingdom of God has come among us.

Meditation: The Christ who spoke and healed invites me to follow in his footsteps.

Like Little Children

Living the Secret of the Kingdom of God

*Therefore, whoever humbles himself like this
child is the greatest in the Kingdom of heaven.*
MATTHEW 18:4

Being a Christian is not an invitation to be sentimental, gullible, naïve, and passive. The opposite is in fact the case. We are invited to love God and others with all our mind and strength.

To be a Christian in an age of doubt takes not only faith, but also courage. To live in dependence on God in a culture that celebrates self-sufficiency takes prophetic resistance. And to live for God in the community of faith requires a courageous commitment of self-denial and the embrace of a solidarity of brotherhood and sisterhood.

Yet, having said all this, the Christian life ought to be characterized by a deep humility. Mother Teresa comments, "One hears so much about personality, maturity, dominance. Instead, the gospel overflows with words like *little children*."[28]

This humility is not weak-mindedness, but a willingness to go God's way and to walk the path of God's upside-down kingdom where forgiveness and not hate, and love and not force reign.

Since our world is more concerned with power than with littleness, and even the church is sometimes more attracted to bigness and influence, the call of the gospel to littleness for the sake of the kingdom of God requires a deep and ongoing conversion for us.

To pray, to trust, to give, and to be generous are all acts of vulnerability rather than acts of power. To serve, to relinquish for the sake of the other, to be available to others without any hope of gaining anything in return—these are some of the ways of reflecting what it means to be little for the sake of the kingdom.

Prayer: Lord, grant me a faith born out of prayer; knowledge graced by wisdom; courage marked by humility; and a heart that loves to do your will. Amen.

Reflection 29

God's Work

Relying on God to Work Through Us

*Moses answered the people, "Do not be afraid.
Stand firm and you will see the deliverance the
LORD will bring you today."*

EXODUS 14:13

Mother Teresa is adamant in her claim that the
work of the Missionaries of Charity is more
than human service to the poor. She writes, "The
work is God's work."[29]

Most of us don't have that kind of confidence.
We often feel that much of our work is an all too
human effort. And we trust that God will bless
what we do.

But not only missionary work can be God's
work. Ordinary work can also be in the service of
God. When we serve those within our families and
befriend and care for our neighbors, we are also
doing God's work. And when our places of work
are in the gambit of God's concern, we also reflect
the heartbeat of the gospel.

Everywhere there are people to love and vulnerable ones to support. And in so many ways we

can bless others even in praying for them. When we are open to God's Spirit and have placed our lives into God's hands, we become channels of hope and peace for others.

Yet it is all too easy for something to become *our* work. Because we put so much effort into our praying, planning, and doing, it is easy for us to begin to think that we are the main players in the service of God. As a result, we can become possessive and protective of our ministry. And so we may exclude others and begin to rely more on our own abilities rather than on God's empowerment through the Spirit.

But we need to remind ourselves that all is from God. He gives us life. God is the One who sustains us. And God is the One who makes our work fruitful and beneficial.

Reflection: While God can and does work sovereignly in human affairs, God also wishes to use us to be a sacrament and sign of his grace.

Emptiness

Learning the Art of Relinquishment

There is a time for everything, and a season for every activity under heaven: . . . a time to search and a time to give up, a time to keep and a time to throw away.

ECCLESIASTES 3:1,6

There is a strange mystery to the life of faith. Its secret is not the blessing of fullness, but the grace of emptiness.

This idea runs counter to our dominant cultural values where the idea of plenty and the pursuit of gaining more are celebrated. Even in our churches, the theme of spiritual much-having is lauded. Emptiness is somehow seen as being synonymous with failure.

But emptiness is a great grace. Mother Teresa reminds us, "If your heart is full of other things you cannot hear the voice of God."[30]

The blessing of emptiness is not passivity or resignation. Instead, it is the art of active relinquishment. It is laying things to one side in order to be more receptive and open to the still, small voice of God's Spirit.

Emptiness is making room for God. In the midst of our cluttered lives, we clear the table. In the midst of the many voices, we wait for the one voice. And in the midst of our much-doing, our hands fall still.

Emptiness has nothing to do with trying to enter a void. Emptiness is not nothingness. It is not blanking things out. In fact, emptiness is quite different in Christian spirituality.

Emptiness is laying our daily concerns to one side so that we may become more fully attentive to God's presence. In making this move, we are not in any way suggesting that our daily concerns are of no importance to God. We are simply acknowledging that these concerns can dominate so much of our lives that we lose perspective.

In the practice of solitude we can become more attentive to God. In this attentiveness the concerns of our life can be viewed in a new light.

Meditation: We may fear emptiness as we may fear hunger. But seeking emptiness that seeks the blessing of God is a great grace.

The Fingerprints of God

*Seeing the Signs of God
in Everyday Life*

> *After this, the word of the LORD came to Abram in
> a vision: "Do not be afraid, Abram. I am your
> shield, your very great reward."*
>
> GENESIS 15:1

Living as Christians in a culture where God is regarded as irrelevant is difficult. We, too, may often feel that God has become absent in our world and in our lives even when we confess that God is with us.

Mother Teresa believes that "not a day passes that there is not some gentle attention from God, a sign of his solicitude."[31]

And she is undoubtedly right! But having this sort of vision of life requires a major refocus. Caught up in the sacred-secular divide we see much of life as secular, and the sacred is seen as the more dramatic interventions of God, such as Abram's experience.

But who is to say that God is not involved in the ordinariness of life? The fact that I am alive.

The blessing of friendships. The safety of home. The challenge of work. The care I experience from others. Is not all of life sacred? And are the little signs of God's goodness not strewn everywhere?

But being able to see the fingerprints of God in daily life does require on our part a particular posture. We obviously won't see anything if we are so busy rushing from one thing to another.

Being able to see the signs of God's presence requires the attentiveness of faith. It comes from a recognition that God is deeply committed in love to sustain and bless our world. One is truly blessed if one can live in this way. For this means that no aspect of life is outside of God's concern, and all of life is to be lived in the light of God's presence.

> *Reflection: So often we do not see for the eyes of faith have become blurred or even blinded. We need the gift of sight to see God's light in the shadows.*

All or Nothing

Living in Radical Surrender
and Obedience

> *Let us fix our eyes on Jesus, the author and per-*
> *fecter of our faith, who for the joy set before him*
> *endured the cross, scorning its shame, and sat*
> *down at the right hand of the throne of God.*
> HEBREWS 12:2

In the life and mission of Jesus, we see someone who was totally committed to doing the will of his heavenly Father. While this commitment was marked by surrender, it was also marked by joy. Jesus lived in the blessing of pleasing God in his kingdom purposes.

We are also invited by Jesus to serve God's purposes. And we are called to do this with glad abandonment.

Mother Teresa saw this joyful commitment in those who came to join her order. She writes, "They want only one thing: It is all or nothing with no compromises."[32]

To be committed to the purposes of God in serving the world does not mean that this is an invitation to a heavy and burdensome lifestyle. God provides bread for the journey, and there is sustenance in obedience.

To be focused on a particular calling or mission or ministry can give our life not only a focus, but also a deep satisfaction and joy.

Obedience to the will of God is never the luxury of the few. It is the daily bread of the many.

The matters of focus and stability are particularly pressing issues for the contemporary church. Since we live in a world that offers us many options and possibilities, including options regarding lifestyle and career, Christians find it hard to give themselves to Christian causes and ministries for any length of time. As a result, many churches have a revolving door. People come in the front door and leave by the back door.

The gift of stability—where we are willing to be committed to church, mission, and ministry through the good and bad times—is a great gift needed for our time. This gift causes us to be willing to make the long journey of service rather than to take the shortcut of convenience.

Prayer: Lord, may I know your will and joyfully obey and serve you. Amen.

REFLECTION 33

God's Hands

Channels of the Grace of God

For we do not preach ourselves, but Jesus Christ as Lord, and ourselves as your servants for Jesus' sake.

2 CORINTHIANS 4:5

We must never assume that God can work in our world in only one way. God can work supernaturally. God can also bless us through the good that others extend to us, whether they are Christians or not.

But God does particularly want to use those who have been blessed by his grace and empowered by his Spirit. The reasons for this are clear. Having experienced the depth of God's forgiveness, the wideness of his love, and the persistence of his grace, they are best placed to speak to others about these good things.

As such we become channels of God's goodness to others. And as Mother Teresa puts it, "We are merely instruments [of God] for service."[33]

This means that we are called both to availability and humility. We do need to give of ourselves to be the hands that God wishes to use. But we also need to remind ourselves constantly that the blessings do not depend on us. We are only a sign and sacrament of the kingdom of God.

Being a sign of the kingdom means that while we are to be a reflection of the grace and goodness of God, we are primarily a pointer, a signpost. In other words, we point away from ourselves, and point to God and his grace, mercy, and healing.

However, in being a sacrament of the kingdom, we are confessing that we are to be an embodiment of God's grace, healing, and renewal. And as such, we are to carry the love of God to others.

While being a sign suggests our limitation and that God is greater than our witness and service, being a sacrament calls us to responsible witness. As a sacrament we celebrate what God has done among us and we invite others to the banquet table.

Reflection: To bless as I have been blessed is the rhythm of the Christian life.

The Icy Fingers of Doubt

When Faith Is Sorely Tested

My flesh and my heart may fail, but God is the strength of my heart and my portion forever.
PSALM 73:26

O ur valiant acts of obedience and service are never merely our own acts. They are simply the signs of God's grace and goodness in our lives. And the costly commitments that we may make for the sake of Christ are the fruit of God's love.

This does not mean that we do not struggle with making our commitments. We can be beset with discouragement and doubt. Mother Teresa admits, "Sometimes I doubted that I have a vocation at all."[34]

So much of what we attempt has to pass through the needle's eye of doubt. We may doubt whether we have adequately discerned God's will and purpose. We may well doubt whether God can really use us. And we frequently doubt whether we have much to give.

But the path of doubt can lead us to the path of trusting God, who takes our doubts and transforms them into a walk of faith. The movement from doubt to trust is never a simple self-evident transition. It is possible that doubt may turn to despair and that in turn may lead to the abandonment of God.

When doubt makes the transition to trust, it is because our doubts have pressed us toward God rather than away from him. We have come to God with our doubts rather than having sulkingly withdrawn.

As a result, the dark places of doubt have not excluded God but have welcomed him. And in time, these dark and difficult places have been illumined by the light of God's presence and have been transformed by his grace.

Meditation: If I have not doubted, maybe I am too confident and self-reliant.

Living in Christ

God Makes His Home with Us

We were therefore buried with him through baptism into death in order that, just as Christ was raised from the dead through the glory of the Father, we too may live a new life.

ROMANS 6:4

In Christ, God has come close to us. And through the Spirit, God has made his home with us. God can hardly come closer!

But what is close cannot only be taken for granted, but can also become so familiar that we no longer have the eyes to see it. We can take God for granted. And we can use Christ as a convenience only when we need forgiveness of sins.

But we are invited daily to live in the presence of Christ and to live our life of work and Sabbath, family and aloneness, and prayer and service sustained by the Christ within us.

Mother Teresa reminds us, "We must be aware of oneness with Christ, as he was aware of oneness with his Father."[35]

This awareness is the fruit of the Spirit but its

ripening calls us to pray in the midst of all our daily activities. It also calls us to the practice of solitude where in stillness we celebrate all that Christ has done for us and we rejoice in his presence with us.

Oneness with Christ is both a gift and an ongoing challenge. It is a gift that Christ dwells within us by faith. It's the miracle working of the Holy Spirit that Jesus lives in us and with us as Lord, Sustainer, and Companion.

But it is also a challenge. We are called to grow in Christ and to live more deeply in him. This involves drawing near, praying, listening, and paying attention to what the Spirit is doing in us and saying to us.

And out of this spirituality we are called to live and serve. Christ sustains our life and empowers us for witness and service. In fact, all that we are and do is because Christ is the inspirational center of our life.

> *Prayer: Lord, may my life be formed by you, sustained by you, and blessed by you, so I may live to your honor and glory.*
> *Amen.*

Reflection 36

A Double Movement

The Joy of Work and Sabbath

Blessed are those whose strength is in you, who have set their hearts on pilgrimage.

PSALM 84:5

Mother Teresa alludes to the double movement of the Christian life: "Take time to play . . . to give."[36]

In our culture we would turn that around. First we give and work and then we may play and rest. Thus rest is always the reward for our hard work. It is what we deserve.

But the gospel invites us to live a very different rhythm of life. It is grace first and then service. It is God's embrace first — then the call to follow him. The first movement of the Christian life is not to serve the neighbor, but to be with the God who has redeemed us. Out of the joy of this friendship, we serve others with gladness of heart.

So we begin life with receiving and move to giving. We begin with rest and move to work. We begin with silence and move to speaking. We begin with prayer and move to service.

In play, we celebrate the extravagance of God's grace. And in serving others, we call them into this extravagance.

It is not easy to live this double movement. The one dimension often tends to dominate. There are those who always seek to do too much and know little of true rest. While there are others who are basically lazy and know little of true service.

What is particularly challenging is to find a rhythm where appropriate attention is given to prayer and work and solitude and proclamation.

Effective work and service can only come out of prayer and the practice of the spiritual disciplines. Yet in our pragmatic age we so much emphasize achievement and productivity that we undermine and neglect the sources from which effective service comes.

Reflection: Let us remember to dance before the world becomes our dreadful burden.

Direction

Prayer As a Source of Wisdom

*So we fasted and petitioned our God about this,
and he answered our prayer.*

EZRA 8:23

Prayer is not always easy for us. We sometimes doubt its value. At other times, we are not all that sure whether God is listening. And more frequently, we are simply too busy to pray.

Our difficulty with prayer is a disturbing sign in our spiritual landscape. This may well reflect the fact that we think we don't need God all that much. We can do things ourselves. Prayer is only the domain of people who are helpless.

But true Christian spirituality has prayer as one of its most basic dimensions. To pray is to befriend God.

While prayer is all about our relationship with God, its riches are diverse and profound. Much comes from prayer, even when we may not feel like praying.

Mother Teresa reminds us that "through prayer you will find out what God wants you to do."[37]

Prayer is placing ourselves open before God so that we may seek his face and hear God's wisdom and direction for our lives. There are many times when we are not sure what we must do. At other times, we have to make important life choices. In all of these situations, we are invited to come to God in prayer.

But we do need to be patient. There is nothing magic about prayer. There are seldom quick answers.

To hear God's wisdom and direction, we often need to become more attentive and to be repentant and open to whatever God may say.

And that is the key. Prayer is not getting God to do what we want. It is listening to what God wants. It is seeking to do his will. And God's will becomes the direction and purpose for our lives.

Thought: Prayer prepares the heart to receive God's purpose and direction for our lives.

Reflection 38

Bearers of Christ

Bringing Christ to Desolate Places

Suppose one of you has a hundred sheep and loses one of them. Does he not leave the ninety-nine in the open country and go after the lost sheep until he finds it?

Luke 15:4

There is a problem in Jesus' story of the good Shepherd. While some may say that it is laudable to go after the one lost sheep, others may think that this is foolish. It's better to sacrifice the one and to take care of what you have.

And so it has always been in the church's long history. Some believe that the heart of the gospel is to take risks on behalf of the needy. Others believe that one should primarily care for those in the community of faith.

It doesn't take much careful thought to realize that these are false dichotomies. One should care for the community of faith. And one should also reach out to bring home to the Father's heart those who wander in the far country.

But all of this can be put much more pointedly.

We should care for the community of faith to empower it for service to the needy.

Mother Teresa speaks of "carrying our Lord to places where he has not walked before."[38] And that precisely is our task as followers of the good Shepherd. Christ invites us to be his voice, hands, and feet. He has delegated us to bring his love to the needy and lost.

This means that the community of faith must always be a risk-taking community that is willing to move beyond the boundaries of safety and security.

Christians must be willing to "be there" for those whom mainstream society may ignore, neglect, or even despise. As such, Christians become a voice for the voiceless, a friend to the neglected, and an advocate for those who are treated unjustly.

While we are called to help in any way we can, the heart of our task is to love and serve in such a way that they may see Jesus—that in their suffering they may see the suffering Christ who gave his life to bring freedom, redemption, and healing for all.

Prayer: Lord, in all of the risks of serving the needy, may we ever reveal you as the Giver of life.

The Power of Love

Practicing Love's Winning Way

> *Love does not delight in evil but rejoices with the*
> *truth. It always protects . . . trusts . . . hopes . . .*
> *perseveres.*
>
> 1 CORINTHIANS 13:6-7

We live in a world of high crime rates, violence, and suicide bombers. Little wonder that we are becoming more fearful, and as a consequence, more self-protective. The stranger is seen as a potential threat, and people who are different from us are viewed with suspicion.

Christians can also buy into these scenarios and embrace the politics of fear. As a result, they too see the world in increasingly darker colors. Evil, rather than hope, becomes the dominant theme.

Mother Teresa, however, raises a very different voice. "Christ's love is always stronger than the evil in the world," she declares.[39]

The point she is making, however, is not simply that Christ resisted the way of retaliation and showed the way of forgiveness. She is also referring to the challenge that the followers of Christ should walk this way of love.

The way of love does not condone evil and wrongdoing. It has nothing to do with being blind about what is happening. Love can see reality for what it is. But love chooses a different way. It responds differently. It seeks to disarm, overcome, and transform. The way of love does not divide the world into perpetrators and victims and so side with one against the other. Instead, love calls for the conversion of all.

Those who are powerful need to be loved into Christ's kingdom as much as the poor. And while the poor may need the love of practical help, the powerful may need the love that challenges them to serve the poor.

In a violent world love may seem very weak. But its power lies in its ability to break the cycle of fear and violence. Love sets us on a different path. This path is Christ's way. And this way can only be walked when the love of Christ fills our lives.

Meditation: Where does love need to grow in the places of fear and anger in my own life?

God's Waiters

Carrying Bread and Wine to Others

Command them [the rich] to do good, to be rich in good deeds and to be generous and willing to share.

1 TIMOTHY 6:18

Many of the church fathers, as well as the Reformer Martin Luther, have made the point that what we have beyond our basic needs does not belong to us. Implicit in this perspective is that one should not go on accumulating wealth, but rather give away what one does not use.

This sounds very strange in our ears. And we, in fact, do the opposite. We do accumulate, and we do so in case there is a crisis and for our security in old age.

While it is appropriate for us to be careful with our money and resources, it is not living the gospel if we only care about ourselves. For everywhere in the pages of Scripture we find the call to generosity.

Mother Teresa makes this practical in ways that echo the Lord's Prayer. She says, "Give them [the poor] through our hands this day their daily bread."[40] In these words, we note the deep spirituality of giving and serving. Here humans become the instruments of answering prayer.

God's way in the world is to work directly through his sovereignty and power. But God also works through us to bring his blessings to others. This is both a privilege and responsibility for us. It is a privilege because we are invited to participate in doing God's good in our world. As witnesses and ambassadors, and as waiters and servants, we are provided many opportunities in the family, neighborhood, and workplace to extend God's kindness to others. It's a privilege to serve God's bread and wine to a hungry and thirsty humanity. But it is also a responsibility. It is sobering to realize that others miss out because we fail to share and be generous.

While the poor especially need bread, both the rich and the poor need the Bread from heaven, Jesus our Lord. Thus we are invited to be waiters for all, so that all might know God's *shalom*.

Reflection: For whom should I be a waiter?

The Bread of Life

Jesus: Source of Life and Wholeness

> *Then Jesus declared, "I am the bread of life. He who comes to me will never go hungry, and he who believes in me will never be thirsty."*
>
> JOHN 6:35

The contemporary church points to the factors of secularism, relativism, and scientism to help explain why Christianity in the West has been in decline. While these factors may well have played a part, the church itself has to take some of the responsibility because it has not been a good hermeneutic of the gospel. In other words, it has failed to live the gospel of Jesus' upside-down kingdom.

This is particularly sad since the gospel is such good news. This is not a gospel of an angry and demanding God. Rather, it is a gospel of the welcoming God. And this welcome is expressed most clearly in the hospitality that God offers. A hospitality that not only sets out a bounteous table, but which offers us the gift of God's nourishing life in Christ. "I am the bread of life," Jesus declares.

Mother Teresa highlights that God comes to us as a gift. She comments, "In each of our lives Jesus comes as the Bread of Life." But she points out that this involves another dimension. She notes, "He also comes as the Hungry One."[41]

That Jesus is the Bread of Life means that he spiritually sustains us by his love and presence. That he is also the Hungry One reflects the mystery of the gospel that what we do to the poorest and least is a service to Christ himself.

This dimension of understanding and living the gospel means that the true worship and following of Christ involves service to the poor. And this has basic implications. It means that the work of care, mercy, and justice is not for the strange few who promote such causes. It is central to the life of every Christian.

Just as all need Christ, whose body was given for us, so all are called to be the servants of Christ and to bless Christ in "being there" for others.

Thought: Christ as Lord of all has need of nothing. But he invites us to bless him in our blessing the poor.

Praying Always

The Ways of the Praying Heart

*And pray in the Spirit on all occasions with all
kinds of prayers and requests.*

EPHESIANS 6:18

Mother Teresa believes that prayer is not simply what we do in the sanctuary, but is a discipline that pervades every aspect of life. She notes, "You can pray at work—work doesn't have to stop prayer, and prayer doesn't have to stop work."[42]

While it is appropriate to pray by withdrawing from all of our normal activities, it is equally appropriate to pray in the midst of life—a life of loving, serving, relaxing, producing, and creating.

Praying in the midst of life should not be a substitute for prayer in the lonely place. But the two can be interrelated. The prayer in the closet is carried into the public square. And the matters of the marketplace become grist for the mill in the place of solitude.

What is of importance here is that prayer is most basic to Christian existence and that we are invited to pray always. This obviously doesn't mean that we can be always on our knees in a particular posture of prayer. Nor are we talking about formal and liturgical prayers.

The always praying is the prayer of the heart. It is mental prayer. In all the many and varied circumstances of life, we lift our thoughts to God to acknowledge his presence, to seek his help, and to pray for others.

Why should we live like that? Is it because prayer is a command? Or is it a necessity? Not really, for there is something much more fundamental. We do so because we love God who has redeemed us in Christ, and we constantly seek his participation and presence in our lives.

This always praying thus flavors the whole of our lives and all we seek to do. In everything we seek God's benediction and blessing.

Reflection: How may I carry the presence of God more fully into the many and varied activities of each day?

REFLECTION 43

Those Interruptions

Listening to God's Gentle Nudges

In Damascus there was a disciple named
Ananias. The Lord called to him in a vision . . .
"Go to the house of Judas on Straight Street and
ask for a man from Tarsus named Saul."
ACTS 9:10-11

There are times when God, as it were, shouts at us. God makes it abundantly clear what he would have us do. These attention grabbers may come in the form of dreams or visions. They may also come in the form of a major crisis.

But more frequently we live with God's gentle nudges. We have a sense that we should do something. Or something or someone is brought across our path.

Mother Teresa speaks of the latter. She comments, "The very fact that God has placed a certain soul in your way is a sign that God wants to do something for her."[43]

This presents a big challenge for us, for it implies the grace of God's interruptions. We may not have prayed. We may not have anticipated.

And we probably do not have the time. But there we are, placed before a person in need.

It is most significant that Mother Teresa does not say that this interruption is "a sign that God wants *you* to do something." She simply says that it is "a sign that God wants to do something." The question for us is, will we stop, do we see, will we join with God in his concern?

The grace of God does not hard press us into service. There is no force or pressure. There is only the nudge, the call, the invitation. God invites us to respond, to serve, to give.

The invitations of God have all sorts of implications for the way we may live our lives. We are called to be open, to be flexible, and to make room. And most basically, we are called away from our pride and cultural captivity to be willing to serve the needy and unkempt stranger.

Since we can't anticipate God's interruptions, we will have to learn to live life much more open-handedly.

Prayer: Lord, grant me the grace to live more attentively to the nudges of your Spirit and to the things that come my way that provide opportunities to serve you in blessing others. Amen.

The Scope of Human Need

Responding to Need's Urgent Cry

> *The poor you will always have with you, but you will not always have me.*
>
> MATTHEW 26:11

Mother Teresa once made the observation that "you can find Calcutta in every part of the world, if you have eyes to see; wherever there are persons who are not loved, not wanted, not cared for—the rejected and forgotten."[44]

This is an important and challenging observation. Often we think that the real needs in our world are in Third World countries. And as a consequence, we cannot see the various forms of poverty around us in the First World.

Not only is poverty very real in the First World, but these nations are also characterized by other forms of poverty. Poverty cannot be thought of simply in physical terms. There are also such conditions as poverty of spirit, of relationship, of community. We may also think of spiritual poverty where worship and prayer have become absent from people's lives.

While recognizing the overgeneralization, it nevertheless appears to be the case that while Third World nations are poor materially, they are often richer in relationships and in spirituality. In the First World there is an abundance of material blessings, but there is a poverty of community and piety.

What this means is that poverty, in its many and various forms, is everywhere with us. And so everywhere there are the opportunities and challenges to love, to care, to give.

Mother Teresa has served us well by saving us from pitying people elsewhere on the globe, while we remain blinded to what is immediately in front of us. Love is always sought for and love can always be given. And need stalks the shantytowns of the Third World as much as the condos of the First World.

This is not to say that all need is the same. And the need of the Third World is a moral shame. But both at home and in other parts of the world, we have opportunities to be God's servants of love and generosity.

Thought: We are sometimes most blind to the needs immediately in front of us.

Forgiveness

Celebrating the Freedom That God Gives

For if you forgive men when they sin against you, your heavenly Father will also forgive you.
MATTHEW 6:14

There is an amazing simplicity about most of the sayings of Mother Teresa. And those who are more cynical might well dismiss some of her advice as being quite simplistic.

At one time she commented, "People ask me what advice I have for a married couple struggling in their relationship. I always answer, 'Pray and forgive'; and to young people who come from violent homes, 'Pray and forgive.'"[45]

In our therapeutic age, we might well smile at the above comments. And we might well think that much more is needed than these simple moves. Don't we also need the psychologist, the sex therapist, or the lawyer?

We might well need this and other help. But we urgently need to recover the healing power of the gospel. As such, Mother Teresa's words echo the timeless truths of Christian good news where the power of forgiveness is celebrated as key to the healing process.

The heart of the Christian message is that God has shown his love for a wayward humanity in the gift of forgiveness. Through the Cross he has opened the way for wandering daughters and sons to come home. In Christ, we have forgiveness of sins through his death on our behalf.

Forgiveness is thus God's power and way in a violent and retaliatory world. Spawned by a love that is beyond our understanding, forgiveness wipes the slate clean.

We are invited to enter into this powerful and strange way. Rather than to blame and accuse, we are invited to show the generosity of our love by forgiving.

This healing way is possible because God has so generously forgiven us. And out of God's forgiveness, we can forgive those who have failed, hurt, and harmed us.

Reflection: Forgiveness is God's strange way in the world. We are invited to enter into it and to practice this mystery.

Spiritual Hunger

Searching for the Living God

*And afterward, I will pour out my Spirit on all
people. Your sons and daughters will prophesy,
your old men will dream dreams, your young
men will see visions.*

JOEL 2:28

The church in the Third World continues to
show a lot of spiritual vitality, even though its
members primarily belong to the poor. The church
in the First World is in trouble. Not only are some
sections of the church wracked by scandals, the
Western church is in decline and is marked by spiritual poverty.

This situation has made some deeply discouraged. But Mother Teresa was not one of these. She
remarked, "Today the world is hungry for God."[46]

While I have no way of substantiating this
claim, I do believe that the present situation is
pregnant with possibilities for faith and spirituality. When the church serves the poor in the way
that Mother Teresa has done, it may regain a general credibility. And when Christians recover the

gift of friendship with those in their neighborhood and workplace and practice hospitality, new bridges can be built for sharing God's good news in Christ.

However, more basic than all of this, God has not abandoned this world. The world is the object of God's love and concern, and the Spirit is ever at work opening hard places.

While in this age of relativism and pluralism the church is regarded as uncool, this is not true of Jesus, nor is it true of the Holy Spirit. Therefore, if we become more fully conformed to Christ, there is the ever-present hope that people will be attracted to the Man from Nazareth who is the Lord of history. Moreover, the Holy Spirit moving among humanity with enlightenment and healing can draw women and men to the Christ who gave his life for all.

In every age there have been the signposts pointing to the God of grace who embraces all who call on him and wish to live in his presence.

Reflection: Where can you see the signs of God's presence in our world?

Strange Teachers

Listening to the Vulnerable Ones

*At that time Jesus said, "I praise you, Father,
Lord of heaven and earth, because you have hidden these things from the wise and learned, and
revealed them to little children."*

MATTHEW 11:25

The God of the Bible is the God who speaks.
God has things to say to humanity. And the
heart of what God wishes to make known is good
news. God speaks to us in whispers of love
reminding us that we can be different through his
transforming grace in Christ.

While God's primary way of speaking to us is
through Scripture enlightened by the Spirit, there
are many other ways in which God seeks to nudge,
encourage, and challenge us. One such way is
through the most unlikely people — the vulnerable ones of the earth.

One might expect that God would use the powerful of this world to be his spokespersons, and
that may well happen. But God most frequently
uses the weak. Mother Teresa recounts the

following story: "One day in Venezuela . . . I went to visit a family . . . [that] had a badly crippled child. I asked the mother, 'What is the child's name?' The mother [said] . . . 'We call him Teacher of Love'"[47]

This is a remarkable statement. So often those with disabilities are seen as a burden. This child was seen not only as a blessing, but as a voice, a spokesperson, a teacher.

So often, those with little power and influence in worldly terms become God's unlikely voices. And there is a reason for this. Their very vulnerability embodies the message: the winsome gentleness of God's love.

While the Sovereign God of this universe can and does command, this is often not his way. God's way is the language of love which does not force but woos us to openness, repentance, transformation, and obedience.

The challenge in all of this for us is to develop a new attentiveness to the way in which God may seek to arrest our attention and to transform us.

Thought: *No human voice is too small and weak to carry the mighty voice of God.*

At Day's End

Surrendering to God the
Things of Each Day

*In your anger do not sin. Do not let the sun go
down while you are still angry, and do not give
the devil a foothold.*

EPHESIANS 4:26-27

There are those who are living idle lives. And
for some, life is marked by boredom and
emptiness. This may be particularly true for the
vulnerable or elderly in our society.

But for many, life is full, often too full. This is
certainly the case for professionals who are
working longer hours.

For many Christians living in urban centers,
there is the busy round of work, children's
schooling, church activities, further professional
development, and recreation. In the midst of all
these activities, there is often little time for reflection and prayer. And after a while, everything just
piles up and we begin to feel lost and over-
whelmed. Clearly, in these circumstances, we are
faced with the challenge to develop a different

rhythm of life—a rhythm that allows us to become more meditative and reflective.

There is nothing easy in busy people developing this new way. But Mother Teresa is helpful in getting us started. "Every night," she says, "make an examination of conscience."[48]

While this has long been an element in the spirituality of the religious orders, this is a practice we can all embrace. At day's end, we can review in God's presence what has been life-giving and what has been death-dealing. What has been good and what has brought grief to the heart of God and to the lives of others.

This review is not a mathematical exam to see how well our grades are. Nor is it an archaeological expedition into our psyche. Nor should this provide us with an opportunity to castigate ourselves. This review is simply an act of humility and prayer: *Lord, here I lay open before you my life and the events of this day.*

Reflection: How may I best build this and other spiritual disciplines into my life?

Caring for the Carers

Pastoral Care for God's Humble Servants

> *After that, [Jesus] poured water into a basin and
> began to wash his disciples' feet, drying them
> with the towel that was wrapped around him.*
> JOHN 13:5

It is most unfortunate that our world has become so deeply divided — First World and Two-thirds World, rich and poor, employed and jobless, carers and those cared for, the well and those with disability.

The impression that we often gain is that the one group has it all, while the others are merely at the receiving end. How out of focus all of this is! The poor also have things to give, and the humble can be our teachers.

One sad consequence of this twisted perspective is not only that we are not open to receive from the poor, but that we fail to see the needs of those who have much. And more particularly, that we fail to care for the carers.

Mother Teresa once commented, "You know . . . my main work is not all this [the many institutions serving the poor]. My concern is my Sisters. If they don't have the right spirit and the right approach, then all our work is in vain."[49]

Not only does this comment recognize the importance of people in a particular ministry, it also highlights the importance of their formation. The quality of a vision can easily deteriorate over time and as more people become involved.

Mother Teresa's observation also highlights the importance of caring for the carers. This is often neglected in church and in church-related institutions. We simply expect that our leaders and workers have the resources to keep giving. But frequently, workers suffer from a lack of encouragement and care.

Following the example of Jesus, who served his disciples, it is important that leaders are there for their workers with help, encouragement, wisdom, nurture, and care.

Thought: Being taken for granted is not only a form of neglect, it is also a form of abuse.

On Behalf of Others

*Carrying Others' Burdens to the
Heart of God*

> O LORD, God of heaven, the great and awesome
> God, who keeps his covenant of love with those
> who love him and obey his commands, let your
> ear be attentive and your eyes open to hear the
> prayer your servant is praying before you day
> and night for your servants, the people of Israel.
> NEHEMIAH 1:5-6

Life has its seasons and cycles. There is the vulnerability of birth and the awesome aloneness of death. There is the passion of youth and the productivity of the years of our strength. There is also the wisdom of our later years and the growing capacity for reflection and relinquishment.

The spiritual life also has its cycles and seasons. Christian growth is no simple straight line. One of the most basic cycles is that of giving and receiving. There are times when we are strong and have much to give. At other times we struggle, we are weak, and we need help and encouragement.

Mother Teresa makes the point that "we have

to pray on behalf of those who do not pray."[50] What this means is that we need to carry the burdens of our brothers and sisters in the community of faith, and also pray on behalf of those who have no faith at all.

We call this intercessory prayer. This is probably the most challenging form of prayer for us. We find it much easier to do things for others. To pray for others, we find more difficult.

There are many reasons why this is so. One reason is that praying for others is an acknowledgment of our inability to help or fix things on behalf of others. Thus, intercessory prayer is an act of humility. In this form of prayer, we surrender ourselves to the sovereignty of God. It is a way of saying, "Lord, we cannot make this happen, but our eyes are upon you."

To pray on behalf of others is not a form of copping out; it is an act of great love.

Prayer: Lord, grant that I may be so open to your Spirit that I may be led to pray for those who are in need. Amen.

REFLECTION 51

God's Providence

Seeing God's Hand in the
Circumstances of Life

Even the sparrow has found a home, and the
swallow a nest for herself, where she may have
her young—a place near your altar, O LORD
Almighty, my King and my God.

PSALM 84:3

In our modern world, because of the power of science and technology, we have gained the impression that we humans can do almost anything. We have also gained the impression that everything depends on us—on our work and intervention.

Now, it is true that we are responsible creatures in God's world and are given the tasks of dreaming, planning, creating, and doing. We have received the mandate to care for and shape the world and to build the human community, families, and institutions.

Being made in God's image, we are called to creative initiative in our world. We are not to be passive and to sit around waiting for life to happen to us. But this call to externalization and to the shaping of our world does not mean that it all depends on us. And it certainly does not all depend on a solo effort.

In nearly all that we are invited to do, we need to work cooperatively with others. Personal responsibility needs to be augmented by cooperation. That is the only way in which we can respond to the many challenges of our world.

But more than human partnership is required. God does not leave us alone in fulfilling our responsibilities. God joins with us. And God is sovereignly at work in our world, even though this is mainly a hidden and mysterious work.

In the midst of life's busyness and challenges, we often do not see this hidden work of God. But often afterward, with the eyes of faith, we can see that God has provided, that God has made a way, and that God has gone before us.

Reflection: In the words of Mother Teresa: "We adore all the designs of your divine providence."[51]

God's Call

The Response of the Obedient Heart

*As he neared Damascus on his journey, suddenly
a light from heaven flashed around him. He fell to
the ground and heard a voice say to him, "Saul,
Saul, why do you persecute me?"*

ACTS 9:3-4

There was a time in church history when God
was regarded as powerful, detached, austere.
Today the pendulum of perspective has almost
swung in the opposite direction. We speak of the
weakness of God, not only of his power. And some
Christians regard God as an accomplice, conver-
sation partner, and a sort of "buddy." While
friendship with God is most appropriate, famil-
iarity is not. We need to remember that we are
mere mortal creatures and that God is the sovereign Lord of time and history.

Mother Teresa makes this practical. She comments, "Let God use you without consulting you."[52]
This is an appropriate reminder for us. This statement reflects an openness and compliance to God.
It reflects a willingness to be used in the purposes

of God. But it also implies that God has a claim on us and can call us to an obedient response.

Here we touch upon God's lordship and sovereignty. And while in Christ we experience God's friendship and love, in Christ we also experience God's challenging call to obedience, surrender, and service.

Living in a democratic age and being used to the practice of negotiation in virtually every aspect of life, we need to be careful that we do not democratize our relationship with God.

He is the Lord. He is not a consultant whose advice we may take or leave. Instead, we are called to live in readiness and availability to do what God wants in honoring him and serving others.

Prayer: Lord, may I have a heart that loves to do your will. Amen.

Small Beginnings

*Planting Small Seeds for the
Kingdom of God*

> He told them another parable: "The kingdom of
> heaven is like a mustard seed, which a man took
> and planted in his field. Though it is the smallest
> of all your seeds, yet when it grows, it is the
> largest of garden plants and becomes a tree, so
> that the birds of the air come and perch in its
> branches."
>
> MATTHEW 13:31-32

Our contemporary world has become enamored with the big, the bright, and the beautiful. Bigness in our culture signifies success.

This thinking has also affected the church. Some people think that only big churches are successful.

However, a more balanced perspective is to recognize that the issue is not the size but the quality of who we are and what we do. Small can be beautiful for God and larger institutions that practice love and care can equally be God-honoring.

But what is more fundamental to this reflection

is to recognize that so many of the beginnings of the works of God and those of his people are ever so small. The theme of the babe in Bethlehem is so often repeated in the way in which Christian ministries have their genesis.

Mother Teresa started her work in the compound of a family in the slums. She notes, "At the first little school I started, on the first day there were five children."[53] In the light of the pressing needs of the mass of humanity in Calcutta, one could hardly imagine a more humble and insignificant beginning. But that is precisely where things must start.

The first few children, the first beggar from the street, the first AIDS patient, these are the small beginnings and the first signs of the kingdom of God's love, peace, and care.

Reflection: In the light of God's call, are we willing to take the first small steps in something beautiful for God?

Love's Praxis

Washing the Feet of the World

*And do not forget to do good and to share with
others, for with such sacrifices God is pleased.*
HEBREWS 13:16

In a simple but powerful metaphor, Mother
Teresa speaks of love's amazing ways in finding
opportunities to serve others. She comments,
"Love has a hem to her garment that reaches the
very dust. It sweeps the stains from the streets and
lanes."[54]

It hardly needs saying that this is no ordinary
love. Love in our contemporary world, while it
may serve family and friends, is largely understood
as self-serving. And contemporary love is more
about comfort than the love of risk-taking and
towel-taking so that we may wash the feet of the
forgotten ones.

This love of which Mother Teresa speaks is a
love that has been birthed by the death and resurrection of Christ and has been tempered by a life
of obedience. It is a love that knows surrender and
has moved beyond self-interest to serving Christ

among the desolate of humanity.

Love's garment, however, should not only wash clean the dark alleys of despair in our inner cities. Its sweep is more universal. The soft whisper of its fabric can bring comfort to any sorrowful brow.

While the people of God are always called especially to care for the needy, the poor, and the vulnerable, God's whispers of love and our gentle hand of service are meant for all within our sphere of contact and influence.

No one is beyond the need for love. All need to be served in a variety of ways. So whether it's a spouse, a son or daughter, a neighbor or colleague, a friend or stranger, let the hem of love's garment extend to all!

Meditation: God cloaks us with the garment of love, forgiveness, and welcome. May we so clothe others!

REFLECTION 55

The Word

A Meditative Reading of Scripture

*Now the Bereans . . . received the message with
great eagerness and examined the Scriptures
every day to see if what Paul said was true.*
ACTS 17:11

It is a sad commentary on much of the Christianity
in our contemporary world, and especially in the
West, that Christians are biblically illiterate. Most
have never read all of the Bible. And many read
parts of Scripture only occasionally.

Yet God's Word is an important part of our spiritual nourishment. While the sacraments and
prayer are also spiritual food, in Scripture, by faith
and through the Spirit, we may learn of the heart
of God, of his promises and covenant, and of his
way with us.

In Scripture we read of the nature of God, the
beginnings of our world, the nature of humanity,
the goodness of God's creative work, the reality of
human waywardness, and the power of God's
reconciling love and grace.

We read of the deliverance in the Exodus story,

of the covenant in the Promised Land, of the failure of kingship, and of the prophetic voice for
justice. We read of the spirituality of the Psalms,
the wisdom of the Proverbs.

And in the newer testament, we hear the
words of the kingdom in the Gospels, the work of
the church in the Epistles, and the word for the
present and end times in the book of Revelation.

Mother Teresa notes, "We know Him better . . . through meditation and the study of the
gospel."[55] Both a reading with the mind and a
reflection with the heart of all that God has
revealed will bring us nourishment, direction, and
hope.

While we wish to reject a mere intellectual form
of Christianity, we also reject a contentless form
of Christianity. And those who serve others, and
particularly the poor, in a world so full of injus-
tice and ambiguity need food for the journey and
guidance for the steps they should take.

*Reflection: Thy Word is a light upon my
path and a lamp for my feet.*

Happy Receivers

Cultivating the Gift of Receptivity

> *So then, just as you received Christ Jesus as Lord,*
> *continue to live in him, rooted and built up in*
> *him.*
>
> Colossians 2:6

Human life begins with receiving the gift of life and the care of parents. Human life ends with the care of others, frequently family and medical personnel. And in between, we receive so much from others: family, friends, teachers, colleagues, and neighbors, and sometimes the unexpected stranger.

In the spiritual life, the story is no different. The story of faith has its beginning in what God has already done in creation, in his care for his Old Testament people, and in the salvation provided in Christ. Faith is birthed within us as a gift of God spawned by the Holy Spirit. And the whole of the Christian journey is premised on receiving God's generous grace and empowerment and receiving from the community of faith of which we are a part.

But even though there is so much generosity and goodness that comes our way, there are times where we experience lack or deprivation. While for the poor this may be aggravated, all of us have needs in our lives.

Regarding this, we need to activate two key words: pray and ask. We are invited to make our needs known to God. And we are encouraged to have the humility to ask others to help us.

Mother Teresa, the extraordinary giver, reminds us, "There is no shame when we need guidance or help."[56]

In fact, it would be true to say that there can be no great giver if one is not open to receive. Receiving precedes giving, just as planting precedes a harvest, and a spring precedes the flowing stream.

> *Reflection: The great gift we need to culti-*
> *vate is, not first of all the gift of generosity,*
> *but the gift of receptivity.*

Abandoned

The Poverty of Relationship

*How can I give you up, Ephraim? How can I
hand you over, Israel? . . . My heart is changed
within me; all my compassion is aroused.*

HOSEA 11:8

Our Western culture is characterized by a poverty of relationships. Our individualism and narcissism have isolated us from each other. And many of our families hang together by frayed threads.

Mother Teresa makes this observation: "Abandonment is awful poverty. There are poor everywhere," she says, "but the deepest poverty is not being loved."[57]

While she has continually brought the challenge to serve the poor, her further challenge has been to create families, communities, and neighborhoods of care. The opposite of being abandoned is to be known, cared for, and loved. This involves being present to the other. This is a form of contemplation. It has to do not with rushing by, but with lingering, noticing, responding, caring.

And being present to, lingering, and noticing means that we will be drawn away from our own preoccupations, and into the world, issues, and needs of the other person. This being drawn to the other involves a minuscule "death" on our part. It is a form of conversion.

Noticing will always call us to some form of response. And here the art of contemplation leads to various forms of praxis, of practical action. One form of praxis is not so much to give things, but to give ourselves in journeying with the other. Thus abandonment is turned into accompaniment. Companions on the road, companions at the table bring the pattern of embrace instead of abandonment.

Thought: The God of the Bible ever turns toward his people, never away. This can become a model for us in the reversal of rejection and lack of care.

REFLECTION 58

The One

Living in, Through, and for Christ

I am the vine; you are the branches. If a man remains in me and I in him, he will bear much fruit; apart from me you can do nothing.

JOHN 15:5

Mother Teresa makes the confession, "I rely on One. There is only One: Jesus."[58] With this she acknowledges both her dependency on Jesus and Jesus' uniqueness and lordship.

In our contemporary milieu this is a startling confession. We would much more readily say there are the many, rather than there is only One. Our pluralistic and multicultural world with its underlying relativism is reluctant to speak of the only One.

In the biblical story, Jesus is the only One. He is the Way, Truth, and Life. In Jesus there is salvation. Through Jesus there is peace with God. But this can never be a mere intellectual profession. This One, the Son of Man and God, is Emmanuel. And it is in him that we live.

To rely on Jesus is not simply to believe that his

death on our behalf will get us to heaven. Rather, it means that we order our lives now by his presence, grace, and empowerment.

To rely on Christ is not simply to live by his example. Instead, it means that Christ and his words and way have become a part of our lives. Christ is within us. This Christo-mysticism means that through the Holy Spirit we are somehow bound to Christ. This has fascinating implications. Bound to Christ means we follow him and are linked to his cause and concerns. And when we ask what these concerns are, we soon discover that Jesus seeks to heal humanity of its waywardness and brokenness.

> *Reflection:* Relying on Christ, we are bound
> to Christ, and as we walk in his way, his life
> will impact others.

The Poor One

The Other As Mirror

Send forth your light and your truth, let them guide me; let them bring me to your holy mountain, to the place where you dwell.

PSALM 43:3

We all have our blind spots. For most, this has to do with our cultural biases. And for many, this also has to do with the idiosyncrasies of our personality. Possibly, one of the places where we are most blind has to do with our abilities. While for some, there is the sense that they lack skills, gifts, and know-how, others are very confident about what they can do and contribute.

What is fascinating is that we often learn things about ourselves when we are placed in unusual and unpredictable circumstances. We also learn things about ourselves when we are with others who challenge us in some way. Thus there are many ways in which light can shine upon us.

But perhaps we are challenged the most when we are with people who are very different. Mother Teresa makes the point, "I have learned from the poor how poor I myself am."[59]

While it is possible that a statement such as this can be a false humility, it can also be something radically opposite. In the face of the one who is so different from me, I can see things about myself that normally would escape my notice.

There are many things we can learn from the poor. One lesson is that we are far too dependent on what we have. Another is that we look down on the poor and thereby exalt ourselves. A further lesson may be that, while we thought the poor person would be bitter, we instead discover that he or she is full of hope.

> *Meditation: If it is so, that the poor of the beatitudes will be filled with good things, then it follows that we not only have things to give to the poor, but that they have things to give to us.*

Future

Celebrating the God
Who Is Ahead of Us

*"I am the Alpha and Omega," says the Lord God,
"who is, and who was, and who is to come, the
Almighty."*

REVELATION 1:8

For some, God belongs to the hoary past, a past full of superstition. Thus these people believe that in the modern world God has become outdated and is, consequently, irrelevant.

But even though God is revealed in the pages of a very ancient book, the Bible, God is the God of the present, even as he was the God of a long gone past. The Scriptures speak of a God who is with us, a very present help in time of trouble.

But God is also the God of the future — he is ahead of us. In light of this, Mother Teresa's observation is most apt: "We must never get into the habit of being preoccupied with the future. There is no reason to do so. God is there."[60]

That God is the God of the future is not only a statement about his omniscience and his sovereignty. Nor is it simply a statement that brings us some assurance in an age of transition and uncertainty. There is more to this seemingly simple phrase. The God who is ahead of us is preparing the way and is calling us forward.

This means that our task is not to bring God to places and into situations. God is already there, preparing the way, beckoning us. Rather, we are called to see the signs of God's presence and to pray for his fuller unveiling.

That God is the God of the future means that there is nowhere God is not. God is the faithful One of the past, the blessed One of the present, and the hoped for and expected One of the future. If there is nowhere God is not, then all of humanity and all of my family and all of my life are safe in his gentle but powerful hands.

Prayer: Lord, may I live faithfully and securely with you, the God who was, is, and is to come. Amen.

The Difficulties of Prayer

Prayer's Problems and Promises

In the same way, the Spirit helps us in our weakness. We do not know what we ought to pray for, but the Spirit himself intercedes for us with groans that words cannot express.

ROMANS 8:26

There is nothing easy or simple about prayer, even though a child can pray and cry out to God.

In fact, there are many difficulties associated with prayer. While there are many problems, including our general lack of prayer, one difficulty relates to knowing how to pray for particular situations. Is it, for example, appropriate to pray God's healing for a friend who has been terribly hurt in an accident, or should we ask God to bring an end to that person's suffering?

Many times, we are not sure how to pray, and sometimes situations and circumstances are so complex and ambiguous that we feel confused. For example, do we pray that perpetrators of acts of violence be caught and punished or do we pray for their conversion and extend forgiveness?

Mother Teresa makes the comment, "If you find it hard to pray, you can say, 'Come Holy Spirit.'"[61] And to extend that in the light of Paul's reflections, we also need the Holy Spirit to give us wisdom regarding *how* to pray.

As a result, sometimes our praying will have to be very general—*O Lord, you know what is best*. At other times, we may pray for God's presence and peace. But at other times, our prayers may be bold and full of faith—*O Lord, we praise you for your healing grace for our friend*.

There are many ways in which the Holy Spirit can inspire us. We may receive the gift of love, or perseverance, or wisdom in our praying. We may receive inspiration where we find ourselves praying in ways we had not expected or anticipated.

The Holy Spirit is never bound and does not fit into any box. The Spirit is light, power, and wisdom. Therefore, in opening ourselves to the Spirit, we are opening ourselves to all that God may do.

Thought: To pray in the Spirit is to be inspired and carried by the very heartbeat of God.

God's Double Movement

The Mystery of Blessing and Relinquishment

*For whoever wants to save his life will lose it, but
whoever loses his life for me and for the gospel
will save it.*

MARK 8:35

It is appropriate to speak of the clarity of God's
revelation in Scripture. But it is equally correct
to speak of the mystery of faith.

There is much in living the Christian life that
has to do with an amazing dialectic. How, for
example, can we be strong in God's purposes when
we are weak and humble? And how can we be
blessed indeed when we give things away?

Mother Teresa touches on something of this
mystery. She writes, be open "to take whatever He
gives, and to give whatever He takes."[62] While
some Christians would want only to stress the former, that of receiving, it is true that God also takes
away.

This ability to receive the goodness and
blessings of God, but also the willingness to live

with open hands before God, is a sign of transformation and humility. The mystery in all of this
is not only that God's giving is a blessing, but that
God's taking is also a blessing.

This taking must not simply be seen as a form
of deprivation or a sign of God's punishment or dis-
pleasure. God may take from us in order to create
an emptiness and hunger in us. We so easily
become possessed by the familiar. We so easily
come to rely on what we have.

To have things taken away by the good hand
of God, while this may trouble and disturb us, may
well become a great grace.

This is the Paschal mystery. Life ends in death.
And of death, life comes. And in Christ's cross there
is the power of the Resurrection.

*Reflection: What may I need to let God
take?*

The God of Patience

Trusting in God's Generous Disposition

> *He does not treat us as our sins deserve or repay*
> *us according to our iniquities.*
>
> PSALM 103:10

There is no way that we should ever take God for granted or presume on his kindness. Nor is it true that God is only generous and kind. God can also be firm with us, discipline us, rebuke us, and even punish us.

Yet, it is true that God in his great love is gracious toward humanity in seeking its redemption and blessing. God is also generous to those who call upon his name and worship, love, and obey him.

It is, therefore, appropriate that Mother Teresa and her missionary sisters should remind us of a basic prayer: "Be to me a patient Jesus, bearing with my faults, looking only to my intention."[63]

The basic motivation of this prayer is not to make excuses about our failings and sins. It is not asking God to turn a blind eye to what needs to be rectified in our lives.

There is something very different at play here. In praying this kind of prayer, we are asking that God will be gracious to us in the process of the change and transformation that needs to occur in our lives. We are saying to God that there are things in our lives that are not holy and good. We are also saying that we desire and seek to be more Christlike. But we are not yet at the point and place where we would like to be. So we ask God to be patient with us. We ask that God may strengthen what is good in us and empower us to overcome all that is displeasing to him.

In this prayer, we are saying to God what we truly desire to be in him and by his grace. But at the same time, in humility, we are acknowledging that we still fall far short.

Prayer: Lord, I do desire to live more fully in you and to reflect to others who you are in your grace and mercy. Help me to grow in your love and strengthen what is weak in me and purify in me what is displeasing to you. Amen.

REFLECTION 64

Above Mediocrity

Finding God's Purpose for Our Lives

> *But the Lord said to Ananias, "Go! This man is*
> *my chosen instrument to carry my name before*
> *the Gentiles and their kings and before the people*
> *of Israel."*
>
> ACTS 9:15

Most of us, with much of our life still before us, have little idea regarding how things will turn out and what we may become. While some may have too high expectations of themselves, others, and possibly many, may set their sights too low.

Mother Teresa seeks to encourage us with the statement, "We must know that we have been created for greater things."[64] But this certainty cannot be based on our own ability and prowess. This knowledge is only something we can possess in faith in the God of surprises.

In history, we read again and again of women and men whom God has blessed and called for his great purposes. And whether we think of a Saint Augustine, Teresa of Avila, or Martin Luther, or of a Mother Teresa or Dietrich Bonhoeffer, we see

God's sculpting hand at work preparing them and surprising them with the tasks and responsibilities that came their way.

But in the final analysis we are not talking only about greatness in the eyes of the world. And we are not talking merely about the great figures of church history. Only some will become great in these ways. Rather, the point is that in God and by his grace and empowered by his Spirit and in responding to his gracious call, we will always be more and different from what we humanly may have expected.

Saul could not have known that he would become the apostle to the Gentiles. And Mother Teresa could not have known that she would become the founder of a new religious order. And you and I do not know what we may yet become through the action of the God of surprises.

Prayer: You know, O God, the way I should take. Show me your way.

Holding Things Lightly

An Obedient Heart Rather Than a Successful Ministry

And we take captive every thought to make it obedient to Christ.

2 Corinthians 10:5

Whether we are aware of it or not, we tend to create hierarchies in the Christian life. And we do this particularly in the areas of spirituality and service.

As a result, we may elevate prayer over the practice of solitude, or we may elevate the work of justice over the practice of charity. Not only is this not helpful, it ruptures the very nature of Christian existence. All of life is to be lived for God's glory and the service of others.

In living this way, it is not only important that we worship and serve, play and produce, witness and pray. It is also important that we live with a spirit of openness and humility and that we hold things lightly. Since God is our home, security, and hope, we need to hold lightly all that we have and do. And this includes our productive and successful ministry.

Mother Teresa makes the sobering observation, "You might be doing great good somewhere, but if you are sent elsewhere, you must be ready to leave."[65]

While the comment reflects the implication of the vow of obedience taken by her sisters, it touches on a more far-reaching truth. This is that obedience to God is more fundamental than our fruitful endeavors.

A consequence of this observation is that there may come a time when God calls us to relinquish an area of ministry when it is doing well. After years of struggle, fruit has finally begun to appear. And suddenly, we are challenged to hand it over, let it go, and walk a new and difficult road in obedience to God.

> *Reflection*: *Beyond our normal securities and beyond that glow of success, God calls us to do his will. And it is there, and there alone, that true security lies.*

REFLECTION 66

The Struggles of Faith

The Purging Hand of Difficulty

> *That is why for Christ's sake, I delight in weak-*
> *nesses, in insults, in hardships, in persecutions, in*
> *difficulties. For when I am weak, then I am*
> *strong.*
>
> 2 CORINTHIANS 12:10

It is both surprising and disconcerting that in certain Christian circles the belief is perpetuated that the blessing of God brings only peace, favorable circumstances, and well-being. This romanticized view of the Christian life is greatly one-sided and fundamentally incorrect.

Yes, the Christian life is lived being held in the grace of God. And yes, there is joy and there are blessings. But the Christian life is also characterized by struggles and difficulties.

Mother Teresa reminds us, "Renunciation, temptations, struggles, persecutions, and all kinds of sacrifices are what surround the soul that has opted for holiness."[66]

She gives us one possible reason why struggles and difficulties are part of the Christian journey.

And here the reference is primarily to the purging hand of God and the world's resistance to righteous living and witness.

But there are many other reasons why difficulties are part of the Christian's story. One is that the Christian continues to be a part of the refractory world. The pain and tragedies of our common existence impact the Christian as well as the unbeliever. We are not magically safeguarded.

A further reason is that Christians are far from perfect. We struggle with our own waywardness and brokenness. As a result, we also create our own problems and difficulties. Our lack of relational skills may resullt in being ostracized for reasons that have nothing to do with our faith.

The wonder of the Christian journey, however, is not the lack of difficulties nor the way difficulties may press in upon us. It is the way God keeps us, in plenty and scarcity, peace and conflict, joy and pain.

Meditation: In times of light and darkness, tranquillity and difficulty, your hand, O God, can hold me fast.

A Small Gift?

Who Knows the Fruit of Small Acts of Service?

I tell you the truth, anyone who gives you a cup of water in my name because you belong to Christ will certainly not lose his reward.

MARK 9:41

While this saying of Jesus in Mark's gospel has in view the reward that those who serve will receive, no matter how small the act of service may be, there are also other ways of thinking about this topic. Mother Teresa notes, "Nothing is little that is done for God."[67] In other words, little is not little in God's eyes. And furthermore, little may produce much.

This is the mystery regarding the way God works. While we may think that God is only interested in using and blessing the big and sacrificial things we offer him, the opposite is in fact the case.

So much of the rhythm of life has little to do with the big and the spectacular. Life has its daily routines and small responsibilities. In the home, we weave a tapestry of small acts of service. In the neighborhood, it is the cord of kindness that gives us credibility, rather than the isolated act of generosity.

And these observations are equally valid for the workplace and for our service in the community of faith. It is much littleness, rather than the occasional big act of service, that is the oil that helps our communities run more smoothly.

However, there is more at play here. It is not simply a matter of the accumulation of what we do. The key melody line is not what we do, but what God does with what we do.

Why is this important? Because not only will our doing never be enough, but more importantly, it is only God by his Spirit who can make things fruitful for his kingdom. It is only God who can make a human act of service fruitful for a spiritual blessing.

Thought: Human good is good. Human good done in faith and prayer looking to God for his blessing is good that will last for eternity.

REFLECTION 68

The Light of Christ

Our Lives As Windows into the Gospel

In him was life, and that life was the light of men.
JOHN 1:4

Mother Teresa was fond of saying we want to make better persons of people whether they be Hindu, Christian, or Buddhist. At other times her statements were stronger, "I've always said that we should help a Hindu become a better Hindu."[68]

What she meant by this was not that her sisters should teach Hindus the Hindu faith, but that through acts of service done in the name of Christ, Hindus would be blessed. She explains, "We do not intend to impose our faith on others. We only expect Christ to reach out with his light and his life in and through us."[69]

This reflects an interesting stance in our pluralist world. On the one hand, this is a position of great tolerance. On the other, this is a position of faith. Here is a love that says no to sharing with pressure and coercion. But a love that says yes to the power of the gospel through acts of love and service.

This leads us to the underlying question regarding how we may be witnesses in our tolerant, multicultural world.

Christians will not all answer this question in the same way. But what is most basic is that God invites us to believe the biblical story, to embody that story as the good news in our own lives, to live out that story in love and service to others, and to tell that story in humility and love to those who wish to hear.

What is most obvious is that we live in a world that is tired of words, particularly words of propaganda. But we also live in a world that is spiritually searching. And those who are willing, for the sake of Christ, to abandon their self-preoccupied lifestyles and give themselves in love and service to others will be light to the world.

Most important is what Christ can do through us as we trust him to make himself known.

Prayer: Lord, help us to be mirrors of your light and love. Amen.

REFLECTION 69

The Holy Spirit

Empowered by God's Renewing Presence

> *Do not get drunk on wine, which leads to*
> *debauchery. Instead, be filled with the Spirit.*
> EPHESIANS 5:18

Living the Christian life, which includes living
a life of service and care to those around us,
has much to do with the effort and energy that we
are willing to put into it. This kind of life does not
just come automatically.

But our own willing and doing is not the basis.
Living the Christian life is rooted in our relationship with the living God. It is a life that is inspired
and sustained by God's living presence.

Thus while the Christian life involves self-effort,
it is much more than mere self-effort. The Christian
life is lived by the grace and mercy of God.

At heart this has to do with the work of God's
Holy Spirit. Mother Teresa notes, "It is the possession of our spirit by the Holy Spirit breathing
into us the plenitude of God."[70] There is nothing
frightening about this, although that may initially
appear to be the case. We want to be self-possessed,

not possessed by someone else. We are fearful about losing control or being out of control.

But to be filled with the Spirit, or to be possessed by the Spirit, does not mean that we suddenly become the passive victims of a powerful force. The Holy Spirit is a person, not a power. And the Holy Spirit does not overpower, but empowers.

The work of the Spirit is to purify us and beautify us from within, so that through the Spirit's gentle transformative presence we desire to please God and to do that which brings God glory.

The Spirit is the dove of peace. The Spirit is the oil of gladness. The Spirit brings to birth the new things of God within our lives.

Thus it is that by that Spirit we are called to live. And to live this way can only bring the love and peace and reconciliation that God desires.

Prayer: Come, Holy Spirit. Amen.

The Gentleness of God

God, the Transforming Lover

I led them with cords of human kindness, with ties of love; I lifted the yoke from their neck and bent down to feed them.

HOSEA 11:4

It is sad to hear that some people think God is really oppressive and dictatorial, and that in the final analysis, God is all about control.

It is even sadder when in probing the reasons for this perspective of God, we hear that this has been gained from a reading of the history of Christianity. The Christian church has not always reflected God's peaceable kingdom.

While this puts God in a bad light, the problem really lies with us and not with God. We have failed to see who God really is and have failed to become converted to his nature and his ways.

Mother Teresa reminds us, "So tender is his love that he will never force himself upon us . . . rather, he draws a soul, God lifts a soul."[71]

There are many indications of the gentleness of God. But the most poignant and powerful is God's self-giving in his Son, Jesus Christ. It is in the babe of Bethlehem and in the man, Christ Jesus, that we see God's desire to reconcile, forgive, heal, and make whole. The whole gospel story is a story of this gentleness.

There is no coercion, only love. There is no force, only love. Jesus did not demand. He welcomed. He invited. He embraced. He forgave. He healed. He set people free.

Since in Christ we can see God's way with us most clearly and most fully, like through a veil that has been ripped open, so we can be confident that God will work with us today.

Reflection: The gentleness of God beckons me, makes me unafraid, and so I run to him.

Double Seeing

*The Contemplation of Christ in the
Eucharist and in the Poor*

*The King will reply, "I tell you the truth, what-
ever you did for one of the least of these brothers
of mine, you did for me."*

MATTHEW 25:40

One of Mother Teresa's famous sayings is that we are "called . . . to see Christ in the appearance of bread, and to see him in the broken bodies of the poor."[72]

This calls for a double act of contemplation and brings together our love of God and love of neighbor, and inseparably links spirituality and service.

Sadly, what belongs together so easily becomes separated. We see the Lord's Supper as a holy act within the sanctuary. And we see serving the poor as part of the work of justice. But we seldom see these two areas as intimately connected.

Drawing her inspiration from Matthew 25 and bringing together the themes of brokenness, Mother Teresa invites us to see spiritual realities and social realities through new eyes.

Broken bread for broken people. Food for those who have no food. The self-giving of Christ so that we may have life. And what we do for Christ in love and service is what we do for the poor.

Seeing Christ can never blind us to the world. In and through him we see the world more clearly. Not as a world to be observed or to be pitied, but as a world to be engaged and transformed.

In the Eucharist we see the humiliation of the Word who brings life, and in the poor we see the humiliated ones who are loved by God and called to freedom and blessing.

In seeing the poor in their alienation, powerlessness, and brokeness, we see the invitation of God that these too are made in his image, these too are made for freedom, these too are called to fullness of life.

The Lord's Supper is food for the soul. But the one nourished by this supper cannot but stretch out the hand that lifts up the needy.

Prayer: Lord, give me the faith to see you in the bread and wine and in those whose marred humanity, nevertheless, reflects your image. Amen.

Joy in Service

The Light of God in Acts of Mercy

*Let us fix our eyes on Jesus the author and per-
fecter of our faith, who for the joy set before him
enduring the cross, scorning its shame, and sat
down at the right hand of the throne of God.*
                                        HEBREWS 12:2

There are many people of differing faiths, or
no faith at all, who are loving and caring to
people in need. Christians do not have sole claims
to kindness and generosity.

Mother Teresa was deeply aware of this. She
notes, "If our actions are just useful actions that
give no joy to the people, our poor people would
never be able to rise up to the call which we want
them to hear, the call to come closer to God."[73]

Embedded in this simple disclosure is a com-
plexity of ideas. The first is that acts of charity need
to be performed in a particular way. And secondly,
doing good to others has at its heart the hope to
bring them closer to the God of life and renewal.

In this statement, Mother Teresa reveals that we
are to be more than social workers or those who

do good to others. We are to be evangelists.

Living in Christ and empowered by his joy, there is to be a certain luminosity about our service. While in our service we seek to be of practical help, we desire that more should happen. And that more is that they may see the face of God.

What this means is that our serving the needy is never to be devoid of joy and of prayer and hope. In the very acts of service we hope that the love of Christ will shine through.

Our acts of service in and of themselves will never guarantee that Christ will be revealed. Therefore service and prayer belong together. In fact, true service is a form of prayer.

Prayer: May my service to the poor and needy be an act of worship to you, O God. And will you, O God, inhabit this kind of worship. Amen.

Self-Examination

Self-Reflection with the Eyes of Faith

> *For by the grace given me I say to every one of
> you: Do not think of yourself more highly than
> you ought, but rather think of yourself with sober
> judgment, in accordance with the measure of faith
> God has given you.*
>
> ROMANS 12:3

Living the Christian life is living a life of ongoing transformation. Our coming to faith is a mere beginning. From that point on, we are invited to know God more fully and to know ourselves more truly.

But self-knowledge and self-awareness can be problematical for many of us. Some are simply too hard on themselves and are forever fault-finding. Others are too easy on themselves and are always excusing what should not be excused.

And between these two extremities lies the difficult gray zone of moral behavior. In this zone we wrestle with questions: Is this what God wants? Is this pleasing to God?

Mother Teresa gives us the following advice,

"Face yourself, with Jesus at your side, and do not be satisfied with just any answer."[74] This is helpful advice because Jesus is both the caring comforter and the light that shatters our darkness.

Moreover, Mother Teresa implies that this cannot be a quick reflection. This requires that we tarry, that we linger. In fact, this process may well become a prayer of the heart where daily we pray that God will show us the way.

Self-reflection with Jesus means that we are not afraid to bring matters of difficulty, darkness, or ambiguity into God's presence. It also means that in the process we are held by God rather than alienated, or that we run away because of guilt, shame, or confusion and uncertainty.

Prayer: Whether I am too positive or too negative about myself, Lord, help me to see myself in the light of your grace. Amen.

The Centrality of Christ

Living by Jesus' Words and Example

> *So we, too, have put our faith in Christ Jesus that
> we may be justified by faith in Christ and not by
> observing the law, because by observing the law
> no one will be justified.*
>
> GALATIANS 2:16

Mother Teresa has made this most basic confession: "The most important thing in my life has been my encounter with Christ."[75]

Millions of others, including myself, can make this confession. Coming to know Jesus, by faith, as Lord and Savior is the most transforming and sustaining experience a person can have.

But how is this possible? one may ask. Jesus lived a long time ago. How can we experience him in the present? Does Jesus mysteriously appear to people?

Responses to these questions are by no means uniform or monochrome. Saint Paul's encounter with Jesus on the Damascus road was certainly different from that of Timothy's. I know of people who have come to faith through a dream in which Jesus appeared to them. That is not my experience. But I am quite sure that Jesus appeared to me as well.

In my case, this happened after a long search and through evangelistic preaching. In that preaching I heard Jesus calling me. And I was convinced that I needed him for my salvation and transformation.

Jesus most often comes to us through Word and Spirit. What I mean by that is that through the gospel empowered by the Spirit, the words of Jesus come home to us as words of truth, revelation, and invitation. And in believing these words, Jesus himself becomes real to us by faith.

However, Jesus can also come to us in the sacraments and in the many and varied circumstances of our lives. Suddenly, and often unexpectedly, Jesus is there, speaking, beckoning, inviting.

Thought: If Jesus is most basic to our lives, then all of our life will be influenced by him.

Looking for the Good

Developing a Forgiving Spirit

Then Peter came to Jesus and asked, "Lord, how many times shall I forgive my brother when he sins against me? Up to seven times?" Jesus answered, "I tell you, not seven times, but seventy-seven times."

MATTHEW 18:21-22

It is reasonable that we expect much of each other within the community of faith. It is appropriate to believe that such a community will be a safe place for us, as well as a place of nurture and care.

However, we need to be careful that we do not expect the impossible and, as a result, become intolerant and judgmental when those within the community of faith fail us in some way. No community of faith is perfect. And Christian community will always need to be characterized by forgiveness and reconciliation.

Mother Teresa makes a practical observation, "Do not be surprised or become preoccupied at each other's failure; rather see and find in each other that which is good, for each one of us is created in the image of God."[76]

This is not so much a call to tolerance. It certainly is not a blanket approval that we can all do whatever we like, even when it hurts others. Rather, this is a call to humility and great generosity of heart and spirit. Just as we will fail others, so others will fail us. And their failure should not be the cause for rejection or indifference or anger.

Instead, something very different should dance into view. The offense or failure should not become the focus of our relationship, but rather forgiveness and seeing the good in the other.

This is an act of faith. It is an act of empowerment because it has in view what is possible rather than what has occurred.

Thought: Seeing the good in the other may well evoke the good in the other.

Contemplation

Fostering an Active Spirituality

*We always carry around in our body the death of
Jesus, so that the life of Jesus may also be
revealed in our body.*

2 CORINTHIANS 4:10

While prayer and the practice of silence
leading to solitude is what we do in our fellowship with God, contemplation is not what we
do, but what happens to us. It is a gift—God's gift.

Mother Teresa hints at this when she comments, "To me, contemplation is not to be shut up
in a dark place, but to allow Jesus to live his passion, love and humility in us, praying with us,
being with us, sanctifying through us."[77]

In contemplation we receive the gift of God's
love and presence with us. We recognize that God
is not only above the heavens, but that God is near.
God has made his dwelling with us. This is a wonderful blessing. In contemplation we do not so
much receive the help of God, but the gift of God
himself, infusing and enlightening us.

Yet this gift is never a gift for mere self-enhancement. It is not a blessing so that we will feel more spiritual or holy. The gift of contemplation is a gift we are to share with the world. The life that is birthed in us is also life for the world. The Bread of Life that is given to us is food for the world. It is light for those in despair and hopelessness.

Contemplation is the revelatory action of the Holy Spirit. It is an infusion. It is being lifted up. It is a foretaste of the age to come when God will be all in all.

Contemplation is not a gift we receive because we are removed from the world. It is a gift we receive because God has drawn close to us, wherever we may be.

> *Reflection: Contemplation has all to do with God's presence. And the presence of God is a presence to be shared.*

REFLECTION 77

The Person

Attentiveness to the Other

When Jesus saw her, he called her forward and said to her, "Woman, you are set free from your infirmity."

LUKE 13:12

One of the remarkable aspects of the gospel is that it has me, the individual person, in view. And while God's concern is with the whole of humanity and with all the aspects of life, including our social structures and institutions, God is also interested and concerned about me.

We see this most clearly in the life and mission of Jesus. Big crowds. Small groups. But also the individual person, noticed, called, and blessed.

The wonder of the Christian experience is not only to know God, but to be known by him. Known, loved, noticed, cared for by God. What an amazing mystery! What a blessing!

This being known and this careful attentiveness that lies at the heart of God's relationship with us is something we should carry over into our relationships with family, friends, neighbors, and the stranger.

Mother Teresa makes the simple comment, "I never think in terms of a crowd, but of individual persons."[78] With this comment, she specifically has mission and service in view. But this has broader implications.

While we do need to think about the larger structures of life and we do need to be attentive to political and social issues, we must not lose the individual person from view. Love, mercy, forgiveness, and justice need to be extended to individuals.

Just as there is a profound personalism that lies at the heart of the biblical story, so a deep personalism must characterize our service to others. The poor and needy need to be helped. But they also need to be known, named, loved.

As a result, Christian service is not simply about helping, but also about friendship. It is not only about doing, but also about embracing.

Thought: Though I am seemingly lost in the crowd, God calls me by name.

Mary

God's Faithful Servant

"I am the Lord's servant," Mary answered, "May it be to me as you have said."

LUKE 1:38

Mary, the mother of Jesus, is a great example for all of us. This humble and unremarkable young girl becomes the bearer of God's greatest secret: the Incarnation. And instead of exclaiming, "Lord, this is all too much for me and this will only bring me trouble and misunderstanding," she says, "Lord be this to me as you will."

Mother Teresa notes, "Mary thought only of how to serve, of how to fulfil her vocation as handmaid of the Lord."[79]

This is a remarkable posture. It is obedience in the face of mystery. It is service in the face of misunderstanding. It is a yes, when a no would have been so understandable. While Mary's yes was all the more remarkable because she brought God's Son, Jesus, into the world, we too are invited to say yes to God's often mysterious call.

Mother Teresa had no way of knowing the

consequences of her yes when she responded to God's call to serve the poorest of the poor. Moreover, she was already faithfully serving God as a nun with a teaching responsibility. Hers could have been an understandable no. Instead, it was a yes.

A yes cannot be one of our own making. A yes can only be a response in faith, and often with trembling and uncertainty, to God's insistent call.

This yes cannot be premised on protection, certainty, and success. It can only be based on trust in the One who has called us.

Such a yes, therefore, calls for the courage of relinquishment: a willingness to let go the familiar world prior to God's call and to enter into the mysterious world of the unfolding of God's will.

> *Reflection: The journey of the mysterious will of God may well be a much safer journey than the journey of our own familiar securities.*

Caring and Healing

*Bringing Transformation
Through Care*

> But everyone who prophecies speaks to men for
> their strengthening, encouragement and comfort.
> 1 CORINTHIANS 14:3

Traditional theology speaks of Christ as exercising the ministry of prophet, priest, and king. In the light of this, the church is called to exercise a rich and varied ministry in the world.

What needs to be noted, however, is that the church as a whole is called to this multi-faceted ministry. No individual person can achieve this, nor can a particular church or para-church organization or religious order.

As a result, some major on teaching, others on medical care, others on the work of justice. Some Christians are effective in evangelism, others in pastoral care, others in business in which they seek to glorify God and bless others.

While many people have celebrated the work of Mother Teresa, she has had her critics. One constant criticism has been her failure to work for changing political and social realities. She is seen as simply dressing the wounds of people who fall over the cliff.

Mother Teresa's response to this criticism is significant. She exclaims, "You change the world. In the meantime, I shall nurse it."[80] With this statement, she is highlighting that we are called to different ministries. And that these are all important. But at the same time, one needs to be faithful to God's particular calling.

It should also be noted that to nurse the world is to work for its transformation. Just as prophecy is not only geared toward the work of justice, but also to the ministry of comfort, so the work of comfort has prophetic implications.

To serve the poorest of the poor is not only to care for them, but it is also making a profound statement. It is saying the poor are important. They cannot be treated as mere human flotsam. They are worthy of love, care, and respect.

> *Thought: Serving the victims of our political and social structures is a critique of the structures and policies that dehumanize people.*

Suffering

A Sign of God's Nearness?

We do not want you to be uninformed, brothers,
about the hardships we suffered in the province of
Asia. . . . But this happened that we might not
rely on ourselves but on God.

2 CORINTHIANS 1:8-9

In our contemporary world, and especially in the West, there is the expectation that suffering can be avoided. We believe that we can live safe, secure, and whole lives.

What comes as a shock to most of us is not only that this is an impossible dream, but that to live safe and secure lives may not be all that good for us. The main difficulty with living such lives is that we can become self-reliant and selfish.

What this means is that suffering may be good for us. Suffering can be the scalpel that roots out our self-sufficiency, deepens our humanity, and places us open for redemptive possibilities.

Mother Teresa is quite sure about all of this. She comments, "Suffering, pain, sorrow, humiliation, feelings of loneliness, are nothing but the kiss of

Jesus."[81] This is a reversal of what many contemporary Christians think. For them the kiss of Jesus is one of healing, blessing, peace, and wholeness.

Where the paradox lies in all of this is that Jesus does want to give us the kiss of healing, but this may have to be preceded by suffering. For it is suffering that so often causes us to see our need. It is suffering that makes us cry out to God.

What all of this means is that we will have to learn to bow the knee before a God whose ways are so different from ours. It is almost as if God can strike a straight blow with a crooked stick. That healing comes through suffering. And the ways of God are upside down to the ways of our world.

Prayer: Lord, in all your unusual ways with
me, including the way of difficulty, may I
ever experience your grace and presence.
Amen.

REFLECTION 81

At Day's End

Practicing Evening's Sacrifice

My eyes stay open through the watches of the night, that I may meditate on your promises.
PSALM 119:148

For so many in our modern world life is so full. And if it is not full enough, we find ways to fill our hours and days.

In the midst of all this busyness there is virtually no time for prayer, reflection, and meditation. Moreover, we are not sure whether these spiritual activities are all that helpful and productive. For us, it is more satisfying to do than to pray.

Mother Teresa's order also knows something about the hard work of serving the poor. But there are also times for prayer and reflection, including at day's end. At the end of each day, she comments, "We have an hour of prayer and of Eucharistic adoration."[82]

This discipline poses a challenge for most of us. And it asks the question, what would our lives look like if the busy businessperson, student, mother, or father would incorporate this discipline into the routine of each day? While it is hard to speculate as to what fruit would be born out of this time with God, I believe it would revolutionize our lives.

Being with God in silence and in solitude, in prayer and in listening to Scripture is embracing a quiet revolution. While nothing specular may initially occur in the form of guidance or ecstasy, this time with God will weave a new rhythm into the very fabric of our being. This time could become the way for representing our day to God. It is the time for unburdening. It is also the place for intimacy and nurture. And it may well be the place of revelation and direction.

While we are ever tempted to do more, we actually need to do less. We need to be more with God and do less for God.

Meditation: God indwells the quiet places in our heart.

The Way

Following the Master

When he has brought out all his own, he goes on ahead of them, and his sheep follow him because they know his voice.

JOHN 10:4

For some, Christianity is a natural part of their lives. They grew up in a Christian home and church. But there is much more to being a Christian than growing up in a Christian environment. And being a Christian is far more than knowing things about the Bible and the history of the Christian church.

The heart of being a Christian is to encounter Christ. This encounter is the work of the Holy Spirit and our response in faith and obedience.

While it is correct to say that being a Christian involves believing that Jesus is the Son of God and Son of Man who died to gain our redemption and transformation, there are some important things that need to be added.

Being a Christian is both believing in Jesus *and* in following him. Mother Teresa explains, "Jesus is . . . the Way — to be walked."[83]

What this means, most basically, is that Jesus becomes a pattern for the way we seek to live our lives. This is the *imitatio Christi*. What Jesus said and did become important for the way in which we seek to conduct ourselves in our day-by-day existence.

Jesus' relationship with God, the Father, becomes important for us. Jesus' care for the poor calls us to do the same. Jesus the reconciler challenges us to be peacemakers. Jesus the healer challenges us in our journey to wholeness.

Thus Jesus is not only our Redeemer, but he calls us to be a small repetition of himself. We are called to become little lights of the great Light, Jesus Christ.

> *Prayer: Lord, may what you did become the*
> *source, inspiration, and pattern for the way*
> *I live my life with family, friends, neighbors,*
> *and even with the stranger and enemy.*
> *Amen.*

REFLECTION 83

An Offense to the Gospel

Freeing the Gospel for Its Transformative Work

Unlike so many, we do not peddle the word of God for profit. On the contrary, in Christ we speak before God with sincerity, like men sent from God.

2 CORINTHIANS 2:17

One constantly hears voices of concern within the church that the world is so resistant to the gospel. And a myriad of reasons are set forth why this is so — relativism, materialism, and scientism have drawn people away from spiritual concerns.

While there is truth in this, it is hardly the whole story. Moreover, this analysis of what has gone wrong is rather convenient. It places all the responsibility on others and none on ourselves.

Mother Teresa believes that part of the problem lies with us — the church. She notes, "Often we Christians constitute the worse obstacle for those who try to become closer to Christ; we often preach a gospel we do not live."[84]

By way of implication, there are many layers to

this penetrating comment. One is the problem of cultural Christianity. Here Christians have so identified Christian values with national interests and cultural values that the gospel has become submerged. With no distinctive message and with an unwillingness to critique dominant cultural values, the voice of the gospel becomes uncertain, hesitant, and eventually mute.

But there are other dimensions. The very things that Christians see as problematical in the world have also come home to roost within the Christian community. Christians have also embraced the good life and pursued materialistic well-being. They are also enamored with science and much of their lifestyle is characterized by relativism.

At heart, Mother Teresa is calling the church to rediscover and live the gospel in its radical simplicity that takes seriously the Sermon on the Mount. To live this gospel the church itself must first hear this gospel and begin to imbibe it.

> *Thought: The gospel always calls and challenges each of us whether we are long-term Christians or atheists or Buddhists. We all need to hear the gospel again and again and be converted.*

Negativity

*The Destructive Force That
Negates the Good*

> *Since no man knows the future, who can tell him
> what is to come.*
>
> ECCLESIASTES 8:7

There is a strange irony to contemporary life, particularly to life in the West. We have so much, and yet we still complain. We have so much power, and yet seem to be so insecure. There is so much that has been given to us and so much that is hopeful about life and its possibilities, and yet we are often so negative.

Mother Teresa makes the comment, "I feel that we too often focus on the negative aspects of life."[85] This is a surprising statement from someone who saw so much poverty and ugliness. And yet instead of only seeing the pain and destructive forces of life, she often spoke of the love, care, and beauty in the small acts of kindness among the poor.

We, on the other hand, who are surrounded by so much that is good, are often given to complaint or negativity. While thankfulness should characterize the lives of so many, a despondency seems to prevail.

To see good in the midst of poverty and difficulty requires the eyes of faith. And to be thankful and rejoicing in the midst of provision also requires a heart of faith.

Negativity so readily becomes the dominant reality when the eye of faith is dimmed and trust ebbs away. When we can no longer see the hand of God in life and we are left to our own devices and to the machinations of others, it is not surprising that negativity becomes the dominant melody of our lives.

But we can live differently by God's grace. We can live in hope. And with the eye of faith we can see the good, dream of possibilities, and give ourselves in costly service so the good may become strong and prevail.

Reflection: Negativity is not a description of reality. It is an attitude to life that can be changed.

REFLECTION 85

Work and Prayer

Work As a Form of Prayer

*So whether you eat or drink or whatever you do,
do it all for the glory of God.*

1 CORINTHIANS 10:31

It is true that work is work and prayer is prayer.
Just as much as it is true that politics is not religion and sexuality is not meditation.

However, for the Christian, parts of life cannot
be segmented, as if those parts have no relevance.
Every aspect of life is to be impacted by the love
of God and the gospel of Christ.

Mother Teresa can, therefore, rightly say, "Our
work is our prayer because we carry it out through
Jesus, and for the sake of Jesus."[86]

In saying this, she is in no way implying that
prayer has become unnecessary and that one
should only work. The Missionaries of Charity
have a strong commitment to times of prayer
throughout the day. But Mother Teresa is implying
that work and prayer are intimately related.

What we learn here is that our work should be
sustained by prayer so that I ask God to empower

me in all that I do. And whether my work is serving the poor, doing home care, or employment at a stock exchange, I seek God's benediction on all my activities. But there is something deeper here and more profound.

Mother Teresa is suggesting that the nature of my work and the way in which I do it can be a form of prayer. So that at day's end I can say, "Here, Lord, is the work of my hands, which I offer to you as a fragrant offering."

This has all sorts of implications. One is that I need to develop a spirituality of work. Another is that my work must contribute to the good in the world. I can hardly offer up to God the work of my hands that has brought about havoc and destruction.

Prayer: Lord, in all that I do may I see your face more clearly and thus serve in ways that truly honor you and bless others. Amen.

Parental Love

Training Children for Life and for Godliness

I prayed for this child, and the LORD has granted me what I asked of him. So now I give him to the LORD.

1 SAMUEL 1:27-28

To be a parent can be a source of great joy. It is also frequently marked by pain. And it is a great responsibility.

This responsibility is worked out within a framework of love, care, protection, teaching, training, and empowerment for life. We desire that our children will grow up to be wholesome, caring, and responsible human beings.

At the same time, as Christian parents we desire that our children will know God and walk in his ways. And in this we are constantly challenged as parents to live godly lives in front of our children. While teaching is important, we recognize the power of example.

What is of growing concern is that Christian parents, particularly in the West, are so committed to helping their children educationally and materially that they are taking away from them the challenge of faith.

Mother Teresa testifies, "My mother loved me so much that later, when I grew up, she joyfully offered me to God."[87]

A parental love that offers up children to the purposes of God is a great love indeed, because it is a love of faith. This is a love that believes that our children will be better off in God's will and in God's calling, whatever that calling may be.

This requires great faith because it is so easy to believe that the securities of our world are more beneficial than the insecurities of faith.

To commit our children to God may well commit them to suffering, and it will certainly commit them to the strange purposes of God.

Reflection: A love that surrenders, rather than holds and protects, may well be the greater love.

Faith

God's Gracious Gift

> *For all have sinned and fall short of the glory of*
> *God, and are justified freely by his grace through*
> *the redemption that came by Christ Jesus.*
> ROMANS 3:23-24

In so many ways faith is a very normal, though special, part of life. We have faith in much of the basic infrastructure of society. We believe that clean water will come out of our taps and that public transportation systems are safe. We also have a basic faith in the medical, educational, economic, and political systems of our society, although there will be times when we will be bitterly disappointed.

But faith is particularly central to religious experience. We have faith that God is there. We have faith that God is loving. And we believe that God loves each of us.

Mother Teresa expresses the belief that "faith is a gift of God."[88] And so it is, for out of ourselves we would never hear God's voice, respond to God in obedience, and live a life that is pleasing to God.

God's gift of faith helps us to see beyond the

mundane and ordinary. It gives us the eyes to see God's presence in our lives and world, even in places and circumstances that are difficult and full of pain.

Faith helps us to look upward, but also to look outward. It helps us to see God as Creator, Redeemer, and Sustainer. But it also causes us to see the traces of God in the lives of friends, neighbors, and strangers.

All of this is not to say that faith is mere idealism. That we look at life through rose-colored glasses. And that we are blind to life's precariousness, sin, oppression, and folly.

No, faith in God does empower us to see life in all its pain and beauty. But it also allows us to see something more. In faith we can see God's action in our world. In faith we believe God for blessing, transformation, and renewal.

Faith breaks open all the places of negativity, fear, and hopelessness because faith is centered in the God who loves and acts and brings the new into being.

Reflection: In faith we pray and serve, believing that the God of all grace will bring hope and healing.

God's Dwelling Place

The Home of the Hungry Heart

That all of them may be one, Father, just as you are in me and I am in you. May they also be in us so that the world may believe that you have sent me.

JOHN 17:21

Being a Christian is not simply a matter of belonging to the church. Nor is it only a matter of believing certain religious truths or doctrines. There is something much more to being a Christian, something much more fundamental.

Possibly, the best way to articulate what this is about is to celebrate the fact that God has chosen to be with us. God has made us his dwelling place. Or in the words of Mother Teresa, "A Christian is a tabernacle of the living God."[89]

God with us and God in us is one of the great mysteries of faith. It is also one of the great joys of human existence. God is with us in many ways. In God's providential care we can see the signs of his presence. But in Christ, God has drawn so close to us. And God indwells us by the Holy Spirit.

God with us is not a statement about our work. And certainly not a factor signaling superiority. God with us does not mean that we now possess certain privileges. There is nothing elitist about any of this. In fact, the very opposite is the case.

God with us and dwelling in us by the Holy Spirit means that we are called to participate in the consolations of God, and also in God's purposes and suffering. God with us means that God is with us as he was with Israel as the covenant God who calls his people to do justly and to love mercy. God with us means that God is with us as he was in the life of Christ: a life of love and service, a life of prayer and healing.

God with us means that God not only blesses and comforts us, but that he calls us to be his heart and hands to the world.

Meditation: Who am I if I am indwelt by God? And how should I then live?

All the Way

Following Where God May Lead Us

> The LORD had said to Abram, "Leave your coun-
> try, your people and your father's household and
> go to the land I will show you."
>
> GENESIS 12:1

Mother Teresa was fond of quoting the advice that her mother gave her: "Put your hand in his hand and walk all the way along with him."[90] Clearly this early advice was taken to heart and was to become characteristic of Mother Teresa's life.

This advice is a challenge for us. We are quite happy to put our hand in God's hand. But for us, this most often means for the purpose of companionship or for comfort. While these dimensions may well have been present in this piece of advice, something quite different is at stake. Comfort is not the main focus, but obedience is.

The challenge for us lies in the phrase, *all the way*. We are quite happy to journey with God, particularly when God accompanies *us*. We are less easy with the idea of journeying with God. We wonder where he will take us. And we are afraid of the hard way. We are afraid of the way of the Cross.

And this is precisely what we see in Mother Teresa's life. Her walk with God did not simply lead her to be a teaching nun in India. It eventually led her on the difficult path of serving the poorest of the poor. This was the way of the Cross.

What is surprising is that the way of the Cross is not simply the way of self-renunciation. It is also the way of joy. Walking with God in his purposes is not the way of death. It is the way of life.

Out of this seemingly hard way comes the fruit of life. The person walking with God along God's pathway is the person protected by God and empowered by God.

Thought: All the way with God is not a scary road. It is the royal road of life.

REFLECTION 90

God's Great Generosity

Living Out of God's Generous Heart

They will celebrate your abundant goodness and joyfully sing of your righteousness.

PSALM 145:7

One of the overwhelming impressions one gains in listening to Mother Teresa's words is that her life was not driven by the needs of people or by the scope of the problem of poverty. Rather, it was driven by love and out of a sense of God's generous heart.

This is surprising. Many who work with the poor question their faith and doubt God's love and care. If God really cared, they say, God would do something to solve the problems of the poor.

This was not Mother Teresa's perspective. She believed that God does care. But God's care is to be expressed through us. We are to become God's generous heart, hands, and feet to serve others. And this commitment of availability comes not from a sense of duty or a need to be needed. It comes from being blessed by God.

Mother Teresa exclaims, "No one spoils as

much as God himself."[91]

As a result, she believed that we can also "spoil" the poor. If God is generous with us, we can be generous with others. If God is forgiving with us, we can wipe clean the slate of people who have offended us.

What all of this highlights is that true service can only come from a place of gratitude, not obligation. Service comes from overflow. Blessed by God, we bless others.

Thus joy rather than duty becomes the key impulse to service. And it is joy that will sustain us while duty will soon become depleted on the long journey of serving the poor.

Prayer: Lord, may I ever serve others out of all that you continue to give me with so much generosity. Amen.

Awe of God

Humbling Ourselves Before the God of Mercy

"Woe to me!" I cried. "I am ruined! For I am a man of unclean lips, and I live among a people of unclean lips, and my eyes have seen the King, the LORD Almighty."

ISAIAH 6:5

While we may wish that it could be all so very different, much of the Christian life is made up of small steps of faith, falterings, the experience of forgiveness, and continuing the journey in faith and trust. There is much here that speaks of ordinariness.

What is good news is that God is also the God of the ordinary. In sleep, work, play, and service, God watches over us. God is not simply the God of the sanctuary, but the God who peppers every dimension of life with his presence.

However, God is not only the God of the ordinary. God is also the One who reveals himself in powerful and extraordinary ways. Mother Teresa explains, "When you come face to face with God, you cannot but know that you are nothing, that you have nothing."[92]

When God confronts us in significant ways, we realize again our humanity, frailty, and vulnerability. We also come face to face with our failures and sinfulness. And we cannot but cry out, "Lord, have mercy."

To encounter God in this way makes the Christian experience so much more than mere participation in religious rituals and ceremonies. It makes the Christian experience deeply personal.

God is not simply an idea. God is not simply a doctrine. God is the living God who draws near to us. God is the God who reveals himself. But God also challenges us. In the light of his love and power, we realize anew who we are. We are mere creatures in need of God's grace and mercy.

In this realization, we are stripped of our faulty notions of self-sufficiency and autonomy. And in humility we bow the knee so that God may be all in all.

Reflection: "Be still and know that I am God," says the Lord.

Rooted in Christ

Living with Christ As the Center

*And I pray that you, being rooted and established
in love, may have power, together with all the
saints, to grasp how wide and long and high and
deep is the love of Christ.*

EPHESIANS 3:17-18

Mother Teresa once made the comment, "In my work, I belong to the whole world. But in my heart, I belong to Christ."[93]

This statement contains a truth that is relevant for many of us. We, too, belong to the world in our neighborhoods, places of work, and spheres of responsibility. Whether we are working in the film industry, in agriculture, in international banking, or in whatever our work responsibilities may be, we are there not simply to earn an income. Nor are we there only to advance ourselves. There, too, as much as in the work of social welfare, we are called to serve, to bless, to do good, to glorify God, to enhance the other, and to build the human community.

What this means is that our orientation is

toward the world. The world is the sphere of human activity and service. It is the place where we live out our faith.

But the world is not the center of our existence. The world is not what gives us the hope and direction for our lives. That comes from Christ, who has impacted us so powerfully that we now seek to live our lives in the world to bring his light, hope, and salvation.

When our hearts belong to Christ, we are also saying that our minds belong to Christ as well as our hands. What we mean by this is that our thinking and values have been impacted by the gospel, and we wish to act in the world as servants of God's kingdom.

But belonging to Jesus is not simply about empowerment for doing God's good in the world. It is also about heart devotion. It is loving the Christ who has saved us and given us new life.

Meditation: In all the places of my heart,
Lord Jesus, may you be the welcome guest.

Indispensable

Recognizing Our Dependency on God's Call and Favor

Before I formed you in the womb I knew you, before you were born I set you apart; I appointed you as a prophet to the nations.

JEREMIAH 1:5

When we are weak and vulnerable, we have little difficulty realizing that we need God's help and blessing. These are the times when we know how to pray.

This sense of vulnerability is usually with us at the beginning of a project. Whether we are starting a family, a ministry to the poor, or a new business, we are aware of all that threatens this new venture. And so we seek God's help, guidance, and benediction.

But when, over time, things go well, we can easily become self-confident and prayer may no longer characterize the basic rhythms of our lives. In fact, we can become downright arrogant. And we can forget the blessings that God has brought our way.

Mother Teresa has faced this. She comments, "None of us is indispensable. God has the means to do all things and to do away with the work of the most capable human being."[94]

This is a sobering perspective. It's a reminder that everything that has been given can be taken away. The one who has much can be stripped bare.

This is not, however, a perspective that presumes the arbitrary nature of God. This rhythm of giving and then taking away is not because the God of the Scriptures is fickle.

Instead, it is a statement about *our* fickleness. We are the ones who vacillate. We cry out to God, and then we ignore him. We beseech God's help, and then pride ourselves on our achievements.

God's stripping process, while it can be seen as a form of punishment, is much more a form of purgation. It is meant to arrest us and convert us so that once again we will see ourselves in the light of God's grace and blessing.

> *Thought: Self-sufficiency will not help our project. It will harm it.*

REFLECTION 94

Voluntary Poverty

*Evangelical Poverty for the Sake
of the Gospel*

> *Jesus looked at him and loved him. "One thing
> you lack," he said. "Go, sell everything you have
> and give to the poor, and you will have treasure in
> heaven. Then come, follow me."*
>
> MARK 10:21

In the missional task, and for the sake of the gospel, we are invited to relinquish much. In cross-cultural mission, we are invited to leave our family of origin and our country in order to identify with the people we are seeking to serve.

Mother Teresa speaks of incarnational mission among the poor. "We are not forced to be poor," she explains. "But we choose to be poor for the love of Jesus Christ, who being rich, became poor for us."[95]

While the call to serve the poorest of the poor may be a particular calling, all of us are invited to acts of relinquishment for the sake of Christ. For some, this may mean curtailing some aspect of their career. For others, this may mean giving the whole of one's life in specific Christian service.

We never quite know what God may ask of us. As a result, we need to hold all things loosely. But what we can be sure of is that God asks us to identify with those we are seeking to serve. We can't serve others well when we are removed from their issues, struggles, and concerns.

Serving others well involves drawing close with an open heart and a listening mind. It involves entering into their concerns in such a way that their concerns become our concerns.

This approach we see so clearly in the life of Jesus Christ. He comes among us. He opens his heart to our struggles and need. He takes upon himself our sin and shame. And he becomes the One who makes us whole.

While we can never fully be Jesus to others, we are called to be his representatives and to do what he did with his help and empowerment.

> *Reflection: Relinquishment is a choice we can make for the sake of Christ and for the well-being of others. Such a choice must be made in faith and in joy.*

Overcoming Bitterness

Responding to the Divine Impulse to Forgive

> See to it that no one misses the grace of God and that no bitter root grows up to cause trouble and defile many.
>
> HEBREWS 11:15

When much is expected of life and of others, we can easily become disappointed. While we attempt to make life safe, it is fundamentally precarious. And while family and friends may seek to serve us well, they do fail us in many ways.

It should not surprise us that disappointment, when allowed to fester, soon turns to bitterness.

For the poor and the marginalized in our world, this is an even greater problem. For when one has nothing or little, and so often one is the victim of oppression, it is not surprising that bitterness ensues.

Mother Teresa is convinced that she knows an antidote. She comments, "Be sure that you have received Jesus. . . . After that, you cannot give your tongue, your thoughts, or your heart to bitterness."[96]

If bitterness is expected in the face of failed hopes and expectations, then it can also be expected that when we access the renewing and purging grace of God that bitterness can give way to forgiveness.

In Christ, we see the face of the forgiving God. All our sins are forgiven for Christ's sake. Having been forgiven much we are to be generous in forgiving others when they fail us.

But even more fully, the Christ within us, formed by the journey of faith, strengthened by fellowship in the community of faith, and sustained by the Holy Spirit, will help us to resist giving way to bitterness and resentment.

Bitterness is discordant and death-dealing. Extending forgiveness to those who harm us is freeing and life-giving. We cannot continue the journey of wholeness in Christ without extending grace to others.

Prayer: Lord, as you have been so gracious and generous with me in your love and forgiveness, may I do likewise to others. Amen.

Faithful to the End

Sustained in the Long Journey of Faith

> *For I am already being poured out like a drink
> offering, and the time has come for my departure.
> I have fought the good fight, I have finished the
> race, I have kept the faith.*
>
> 2 TIMOTHY 4:6-7

We live in a culture of fragile loyalties. The idea of making long-lasting commitments is difficult for us. And we see the effects of this in marriages, families, businesses, and our political institutions.

We also see this in our churches. Many churches have the proverbial revolving door. People join the church. But also many leave by the back door. Even in the realm of religious faith, people now wish to keep their options open. Maybe all faiths are equally salvific, many people claim.

Mother Teresa provides a very different perspective. While she is open to all other faiths, she is clear about her Christian beliefs. And while she has been flexible in her journey of faith, she is strong about the commitments she has made. She comments, "I would be disposed to renounce my life rather than my faith."[97] This is a strong assertion. But it shows what lies at the core of this remarkable woman.

This poses a challenge for us. Is our faith so important and so deep? And how can it grow so we also can be deeply rooted in Christ?

Faith grows and deepens in many ways. But at its core, it can only grow because God is holding and nurturing us and we continue to respond to God in faith and obedience.

We grow in Christ through a relationship with him who gave his life for us and who offers us the gift of new life. This relationship is sustained by the work of the Holy Spirit, and on our side, by a life of prayer and receptivity to all that God would say to us.

But we grow not only by praying, but also by serving. In doing the works of Christ in our deeply wounded world, our lives are deepened by the Christ who upholds us and grows within us.

Reflection: Our final commitment may be, Lord, to whom else shall we turn? You alone have the words of eternal life.

In Silence

Listening to the God Who Speaks

I wait for the LORD, my soul waits, and in his word I put my hope. My soul waits for the Lord more than watchmen wait for the morning.

PSALM 130:5-6

It is surprising that Mother Teresa, as a person who speaks so much about service to the poor, also had so much to say about meditation, solitude, and prayer. And it is almost as if the latter is more significant for her. For it is out of contemplation that the heart speaks and the hand serves.

Why all of this is surprising is that we have activists who don't pray and contemplatives who do not do the work of justice. With Mother Teresa we have an emphasis on both, and both activities are seen as interrelated.

But she always returns to the theme of silence. She notes, "Jesus always waits for us in silence. In silence he listens to us; in silence he speaks to our souls. In silence we are granted the privilege of listening to his voice."[98]

This theme has particular relevance for us

moderns who are generally so busy that we are afraid of slowing down. And we are even more afraid of the practice of silence and solitude.

Its relevance lies in the fact that this may be one step toward the much-needed renewal of Christian spirituality in the Western church. This church, often so busy, is so bereft of the power of the gospel.

To live in God and with God in a deeply reflective and meditative silence, in order to be attentive to God and the workings of God in our inner being, is a way to live the Christian life in a centered way. Living this way we can contribute to the life together in Christian community and live God's life in the world that is winsome, marked by humility, and empowered by the Spirit.

Thought: We claim so often that God does not speak. What is more to the point is that we usually do not listen.

Greatness?

True Humility and True Greatness

> *Jesus called them together and said, "You know that the rulers of the Gentiles lord it over them, and their high officials exercise authority over them. Not so with you. Instead, whoever wants to become great among you must be your servant."*
> MATTHEW 20:25-26

God is great. And God's greatness, while it also lies in his power, is more basically a greatness of love and grace. God is the Suffering One who has come to give us new life.

There are also great people. Poets. Scientists. Politicians. Musicians. Philosophers. In every sphere of life, there are people who have made outstanding contributions to human welfare. And in the life of the church there are the prophets, the martyrs, and the saints. These have been shining examples of the passion, grace, and goodness of God.

Mother Teresa was frequently asked if she was a saint. This was her typical response: "Oh no; every person was created to become a saint. . . . We were created for great things. God manifests his greatness by using our nothingness. . . . I am happy that you see Jesus in me, because I see him in you."[99]

Being a saint is not some special status that we have achieved by our own doing. Being saintly has to do with the outworking of the grace and purposes of God in our lives. It is the love of Christ growing within us and captivating us in such a way that we begin to live that love toward others in ever-increasing ways.

Furthermore, being a saint is not the preoccupation of the saint. The saint is concerned about knowing God, doing the will of God, and serving the purposes of God in our world.

Thus the focus is not us. It is all about God and what God wishes to do through us.

Thought: The saint is unmindful of self, but focused on the living God.

Vocation

Servanthood Rather than Career

It is the Lord Christ you are serving.
COLOSSIANS 3:24

Christians are encouraged to work in every sphere of life—in the home, in politics, in the media, in business, in the arts, in social welfare. They are encouraged to engage the whole gamut of human activity in order to be salt and light. They are there not simply for themselves, nor only for the business in which they are engaged. They are there for God.

This grand vision flows out of the belief that the salvation that God calls us into completely reorients the direction of our lives. Redemption through faith in Christ does not only bless us, it also calls us to new priorities. We now live for God to do God's will in the world.

As a result, the will of God becomes our first priority. Therefore, Mother Teresa can say to the members of her order, "Your vocation is not to work for the lepers. Your vocation is to belong to Jesus. The work for the lepers is only your love for

Christ in action."[100]

This has implications for the way in which we view our life in the world. While the pressure will always be for us to conform ourselves to the way of the world, to work to further our career, ambition, and status, the way of God is different. Our vocation is not our career. Our vocation is to be the servants of Christ. And we seek to work out this servanthood in whatever sphere of life God has called us.

What this means is that I am a Christian first and foremost, and then I am a lawyer, homemaker, mechanic, farmer, or educator.

This is a wonderfully exciting and challenging way to live. Here the service of God is primary. So whether we serve God as pastors, researchers, social welfare workers, artists, or missionaries, the challenge for us is to serve God and bless those around us.

> *Prayer: Lord, it is ever so easy for me to get lost in my work and in my many other responsibilities so that you are no longer the central focus. Renew my vision to serve you in all I do. Amen.*

Spiritual Disciplines

Creating Rhythms for the Spiritual Life

> *In the night I remember your name, O LORD, and
> I will keep your law. This has been my practice: I
> obey your precepts.*
>
> PSALM 119:55-56

While the work of the Holy Spirit is linked to
Word and sacrament, the Spirit works cre-
atively and mysteriously in the human heart, in the
community of faith, and in the world. It is thus the
privilege of the Christian to be open to the
renewing and empowering work of the Spirit.

But the spiritual life is not simply sustained by
the mysterious workings of the Spirit. It is also sustained by the community of faith of which we are
a part and by the spiritual disciplines that are a part
of our daily lives.

Some of these are well-known and widely
practiced. Prayer is one that is most common.
Fasting is less practiced in the Western church.

Besides these and other disciplines, Mother
Teresa has created some of her own and these
have become part of her order. She speaks of the

spiritual practice of the "silence of the tongue, by praising God and speaking the life-giving Word of God that is the Truth, that enlightens and inspires, brings peace, hope and joy."[101]

In practicing this spiritual discipline we use our speaking to edify, bless, instruct, guide, and heal. Our speaking is not to harm, retaliate, scorn, or destroy.

This poses a challenge for us because it puts the searchlight first and foremost not on our speaking, but on what is in our hearts. Words that bless come from a heart that loves. Thus the heart of the matter is the conversion of the heart by the grace of God. And from a heart filled with the goodness of God will come words that bring healing and hope.

But this inspiration needs the gentle harness of the spiritual disciplines. Thus we commit and orient ourselves to speak in ways that build up and make whole.

Reflection: The spiritual disciplines are not the source of the river. They are merely its banks.

Proclamation

Winsomely Retelling the Gospel Story

*But when the time had fully come, God sent his
Son, born of a woman, born under the law, to
redeem those under the law, that we might receive
the full rights of sons.*

GALATIANS 4:4-5

In the West, Christians have become uncertain
about sharing their faith with others through
telling the gospel story. We have become more
comfortable with doing the acts of mercy than with
sharing the good news of what God has done in
Christ.

There are many reasons for this reluctance. One
has to do with our multicultural world which,
characterized by tolerance, sees witness to one's
particular faith as a form of unacceptable prose-
lytism. Another stems from the failure of Christians
to deeply indwell the biblical story. As a result, that
story has not sufficiently penetrated our lives to
make it worth telling.

While Mother Teresa has always stressed that
her Missionaries of Charity should proclaim the

good news through acts of service to the poorest of the poor, she also believes that "Jesus . . . [is] the Truth—to be told."[102] This is important. And we need to recapture the art of gossiping the gospel.

This is best done not simply in special events organized by the church, but in the rhythm of daily life of the church's members. At work, in the neighborhood, on the playground, and in the normal activities of life, we have the opportunity to both listen to and speak to those with whom we come in contact.

When Jesus is both the Life to be lived as well as the Truth to be told, our witness will have integrity. And this witness may well become more telling when telling occurs within the framework of hospitality, welcome, and service.

Thought: Christians need to recover their voice. And when the first voice is the voice of worship and praise, the second can be one of joyful witness.

Giving

The Surprise of Receiving

He who gives to the poor will lack nothing, but he who closes his eyes to them receives many curses.
PROVERBS 28:27

If one were to listen to many of the dominant voices in our Western world, one would think that taking was the greatest virtue. We take from the earth without careful thought to its vulnerability and its limitation. We take from the Third World without careful thought to the vision of economic justice. We take from the market to exploit it for our own ends. And we take from each other in order to enhance ourselves.

But taking can never be the moral heartbeat of the universe. Giving is, finally, what brings life.

Mother Teresa was fond of quoting the prayer of Saint Francis, ". . . It is in giving that we receive."[103] It is clear that she not only prayed this, but she lived it.

And we are invited to live the same, for this strange idea was not the brainchild of the mystical and visionary Saint Francis, but this vision lies at the heart of the biblical story.

In Creation, God gave. In the garden, God gave the woman to the man. In Exodus, God gave liberation. In the Promised Land, he gave the covenant. In times of distress, he gave judges. In times of religious apostasy, God gave the prophets. And in the fullness of time, God gave his beloved Son as Savior of humanity. And at Pentecost, God gave the Spirit.

Throughout history, God has endowed women and men with a variety of gifts to bring leadership, nurture, teaching, worship, and healing.

In conversion, God gives us himself. In repentance God gives us forgiveness. In pain, God gives us transformation. In the sacraments, God gives us new life.

The God who gives invites us to give ourselves to him, and to give ourselves to each other in love and to the stranger in need.

Meditation: In following the God who gives,
we are given new life.

Special Callings

Living Our Vocation in the World

You must go to everyone I send you to and say whatever I command you. Do not be afraid of them, for I am with you.

JEREMIAH 1:7-8

Mother Teresa believes that people are specially called by God to perform particular tasks and ministries. She herself was specially called to serve the poorest of the poor. She comments, "All of us are called to belong to God. But some of you are called in a special way to the priesthood and the religious life."[104]

There is little doubt that in being willing to live a life of chastity, poverty, obedience, and service, as is the case with the Missionaries of Charity, that a special call is needed. But for the Christian, a special call is needed in whatever way we are called to be and serve in the world.

To be a priest or a politician, a pastor or an artist, a missionary or an economist, should be as a result of the purposes of God in our lives, not simply as a career choice.

So how does this call come to us? A call presupposes a posture of waiting. One waits for the call to come. One waits for God to speak. This is difficult for us. We do not like waiting. We have to get on with life. We have to make choices. We have to get on with our careers. We are people in a hurry. The busyness and restless activity of our world draws us in. And life, we think, is all about being proactive and being self-assertive.

But calling presupposes waiting and listening. This listening is with a heart that longs to do God's will. It is a listening of the obedient heart.

However, callings lie in the realm of God's sovereignty. Why God calls one person to be a prophet and another a businessperson is the mystery of God that we must all embrace.

Prayer: Lord, waiting and listening are hard for me. I so often do what I wish to do and I hope that you are with me in my doing. Change my heart, O Lord, that I may seek what you want to give and how you want to direct. Amen.

Disappointment

Bearing the Pain of Failure

> *Therefore, you will see the land only from a distance; you will not enter the land I am giving to the people of Israel.*
>
> DEUTERONOMY 32:52

It is evident from reading the words of Mother Teresa and listening to her biographers that she was a woman of positive action, joy, and hope. This does not mean that she was a stranger to suffering and disappointment.

One disappointment was that, while Mother Teresa and her sisters were committed to a downward mobility for the sake of Christ, this was not always true of those that were helped. Mother Teresa laments, "When we succeed in educating a child, he goes to live in better surroundings, and the slum people remain without any leader able to uplift them."[105]

This is a frequent concern of those involved in incarnational mission and ministry. Those who have much are willing to lay this aside for the sake of the gospel, while those among the poor who are blessed by their ministry so often seek to clamber toward the resources and riches that the missioners have left behind.

This can be a painful trial for those who seek to serve among the poor. And while the temptation may be to criticize or to give up, service to the poor should continue in fidelity to the gospel.

All of this shows us that faithful service is not without pain and disappointment. To be doing God's will does not mean one will experience magical protection and unending blessing. Even those who please God in their faithful service may also be called to suffering. No one was more faithful in serving the Father than Jesus. Yet he, too, was rejected and suffered, and many he healed even failed to give thanks.

Reflection: The cost of faithful service may include carrying the pain of disappointment.

REFLECTION 105

The Ascetic Ideal

Calling, Charisma, and Relinquishment

> *Is not this the kind of fasting I have chosen: to loose the chains of injustice and untie the cords of the yoke, to set the oppressed free and break every yoke? Is it not to share your food with the hungry and to provide the poor wanderer with shelter?*
> ISAIAH 58:6-7

Throughout the long biblical story there pulsates the theme of God's love and care for humanity and God's concern for the needy and the poor.

We should never attempt to play the one theme off against the other. God's concern for the poor does not mean that God is not concerned for all. But God's concern for the poor needs to be heard again and again, for the poor we may pity but also neglect.

In the Pentateuch, we constantly read that the people of Israel were especially to be mindful of the poor for they themselves were the rescued oppressed slaves from Egypt. And in the Prophets, Israel's relationship with God was measured by their care for the poor and their pursuit of justice.

These themes of care for the poor were embedded in the life and mission of Jesus and in the practice of the early church. And throughout the church's long march in history, care for the poor remains a compelling mantra. But it was a calling that the church practiced and had to be called back to again and again.

Mother Teresa and her sisters embody that call. And in living that call in true fidelity, they themselves embrace a life of poverty. This is showing true love for the poor by a mission that deeply identifies with the poor. And it was this vision Mother Teresa was so concerned to maintain. She tells us we have to resist "love of comfort that would lead us to choose a comfortable and insignificant mediocrity."[106]

Thought: In so many countries the church has become a comfortable middle class organization. It needs to hear again the gospel call to serve the least for the sake of the kingdom.

Re-Evangelization

Sharing the Good News with Those Who Have Wandered

*Be merciful to those who doubt; snatch others
from the fire and save them; to others show
mercy.*

JUDE 22-23

Mother Teresa was all too aware of the way in which Christianity has lost ground in the Western world. She comments, "The Gospel needs to be brought back to the countries falling away from Christianity."[107]

This is a huge challenge. And the pressing question is how may that best be done? While there are no simplistic answers, one place to start is to note how it should not be done.

There is little point for Christians to pine for a return to the good old days when Christianity was more dominant in Western culture. Furthermore, there is little point in blaming the Enlightenment or science or technology or urbanization.

The way forward is both to recognize that the church in the past has also failed and that the present difficulty may well be a blessing in disguise. Let me develop this latter idea.

In a context of skepticism and disregard and the ever-increasing marginalization of the church in the West, there is a new opportunity for the church, stripped of a previous power and influence, to exercise the power of authentically living the gospel.

A humbled church, like the humiliated Christ, may be able to be a greater witness in our world than the church as the guardian of Christendom. Thus the contemporary church needs to accept its present marginal status as a purgation from God's hand. And in ever-deeper conversion, move from being a church of consumer Christianity to being God's worshiping and serving people who are willing to live the Sermon on the Mount.

The easy gospel will never convert the West and other countries on the globe that are forsaking the faith. It is only a church that lives the power of the gospel that will be listened to.

Prayer: Lord, help us, as your people, to enter more fully into your love, your Word, and the power of your Spirit. Amen.

Fullness

Living in Fellowship with Father, Son, and Holy Spirit

My purpose is that they may be encouraged in heart and united in love, so that they may have the full riches of complete understanding, in order that they may know the mystery of God, namely, Christ, in whom are hidden all the treasures of wisdom and knowledge.

COLOSSIANS 2:2-3

The good news of God's story is that God reaches toward us with his love and grace to welcome us into a living relationship with him. The Christian journey is the deepening of this relationship. Mother Teresa expresses this in a prayer to God: "Penetrate and possess our whole being."[108]

In the language of Christian spirituality this is growth in our union with God. Or in more evangelical language, this has to do with growing in maturity in Christ. What this means is that the purpose of the Christian life is never simply in the direction of service and ministry alone. It also moves in the direction of becoming more

Christlike. This inner and outer movement, or in other words, this movement toward God and neighbor, is central to Christian spirituality.

For Mother Teresa the movement is not an orientation toward Christ only to better serve the neighbor. No, we need to be first and foremost oriented toward Christ to become more Christlike. Christ is not some means to an end. Christ is Savior and Lord and we need to live in him.

Moreover, serving the neighbor is a form of worshiping Christ. We serve the other for his sake.

Thus growth in our relationship with God has many dimensions. It is growth of head, heart, and hand. It is growth in the knowledge of God, in the practice of the spiritual disciplines, and in loving service to others.

It is also growth in fellowship. Being in fellowship with Father, Son, and Holy Spirit invites us into fellowship with brothers and sisters in the community of faith and with the neighbor, the stranger, and the poor.

> *Thought*: *Growth in God will always mean growth in the love and care for others.*

Surrender

Putting All in God's Hands

Then he called the crowd to him along with his disciples and said: "If anyone would come after me, he must deny himself and take up his cross and follow me."

MARK 8:34

It is true that so often we turn things in such a way that we become the center of things—everything has to do with us and has to be for our own benefit. This can also occur in our relationships with each other. And as such, these relationships will become destructive.

But this can also occur in our relationship with God. The vision that God is for me gets twisted into the perspective that God is there simply for my benefit. This really has the cart before the horse. The biblical vision is that I exist for God, not that God is there for me. So the first question is not "Lord, how can you bless me," but, "Lord, how may I honor and obey you."

Mother Teresa has grappled with this. She notes, "To belong fully to God we have to give up everything."[109]

This is another way of saying that it is all about God. God is central. God is to be honored and glorified. And belonging fully to God is to be caught up in God's kingdom and his concerns. It is also saying something else which cuts close to the bone of our contemporary culture. The culture says it's all about me and about getting more. The gospel says it's all about God and about relinquishment.

For God to be central, our own idols have to be demolished. If we are to live in God, we can't also live in our own strength and self-determination. And if we are to live for God, our own preoccupations have to be relegated to the purposes of God's kingdom.

This is the narrow way of the gospel. While there is nothing narrow about God's love and generosity, there is a narrow way of obedience. Here, our yes to God becomes a no to other things, particularly our own way.

> *Reflection: The Christ who gave us life out of his cross also lays a cross upon us. Life and a cross are both given to us. Forgiveness offered and obedience called for are equally the contours of the Christian life.*

Faithfulness

Living Our God-Given Charism

There are different kinds of gifts, but the same Spirit. There are different kinds of service, but the same Lord.

1 CORINTHIANS 12:4-5

In the sphere of Christian service there is the tendency constantly to do more and more. In many ways this is commendable. There is much to be done and human need has no limits. And so one program of help and intervention leads to another.

But this also has its problems. The more we try to do, the more we may overextend our resources and sometimes our abilities.

There are other problems as well. The attempt to do more may come out of our notions of grandeur, rather than out of a desire to respond more fully to people's needs. Or it may come out of an inability to say no.

But more fundamentally, attempting to do more and more and to expand a ministry in all directions may take us away from what God has asked us to do. We begin something by responding to God's call and we end up deciding ourselves what we want to do.

Mother Teresa is very clear that we should remain faithful to the charism that the Spirit has given. She counsels, "No Missionary of Charity must drift away from the humble works [of serving the poorest of the poor], because these are the works nobody will do."[110]

Over the years, many have sought to advise Mother Teresa about what *else* she should do. She steadfastly refused. And she has done this out of a sense that this violates God's calling.

Faithfulness to God's initial calling is not only an act of great humility (because surely we can successfully do more, so we think), but it is also a response to God's sovereignty. This is what God asks of us and we will be faithful to this task!

> *Prayer: In seeing the way you have gifted us, O Lord, help us to further see what we should do and what we should say no to.*
> *Amen.*

Signs of the Kingdom

Proclamation, Healing, Works of Mercy

> *So he replied to the messengers, "Go back and report to John what you have seen and heard: The blind receive sight, the lame walk, those who have leprosy are cured, the deaf hear, the dead are raised, and the good news is preached to the poor."*
>
> LUKE 7:22

All through God's long march with humanity it is evident that God wanted to bring salvation and wholeness to humankind and to call into being a people who would reflect the grace and goodness of God. This comes to particular fulfillment in the person and work of Jesus Christ.

Jesus, Son of Man, Son of God, and faithful servant of the kingdom of God, proclaims good news, heals the sick, and becomes the hope of the poor. In his life and ministry we gain a window into the heart of God and a visible demonstration of what God's kingdom concerns are all about.

The people of faith, empowered by the Spirit, are to continue the mission of Jesus. They, too, are to proclaim good news and be the instruments of healing and transformation. And they, too, are called to serve the poor.

In all of this, it is important to hear Mother Teresa's concern, "People are attracted by what they see rather than by what they hear."[111]

The challenge facing contemporary Christians is that so often there are many words, but little in terms of a lifestyle that reflects the values of the kingdom and a service that exhibits God's great love for humanity. It is of little wonder that, for many, Christianity is not all that attractive.

Our world is tired of words, particularly of clichéd religious answers and empty political promises. But what is winsome and attractive is love in action. A love spawned by God that sweeps us up in its intensity and transformative power and, as such, so captivates us that we begin to live this love in serving others. This is powerfully attractive.

In a world of new "tribal" animosities and new polarizations of hatred and fear, there are new opportunities for Christians to show Christ's way—a way of love and peace.

> *Reflection: Again in our day, it is impera-tive that Christians walk and serve in the way of Christ rather than in the national-ism and ideologies of our time.*

Reflection III

Confession

Seeking God's Gracious Pardon

> *But he was pierced for our transgressions, he was*
> *crushed for our iniquities; the punishment that*
> *brought us peace was upon him, and by his*
> *wounds we are healed.*
>
> ISAIAH 53:5

The God of the Bible is the Creator God who
has called all things into being and who sustains all things by his power. But this God is also
the God who redeems and heals.

As the Redeeming God, God is the Suffering
One. God suffers as a result of human disobedi-
ence and sin. And instead of reacting in anger and
withdrawal, God engages our folly and waywardness and makes a way of forgiveness for us.

Our sinful wrongdoing never remains simply
at the horizontal level. It also has a primary ver-
tical dimension. When I do violence to another
human being, I am also doing violence to the God
who has made all of us in his image and who calls
me to love even the enemy.

As a result, confession of our sins to God is

central to Christian spirituality. Mother Teresa reminds us, "Let us often say during the day, 'Lord wash away my sin and cleanse me from all my iniquity.'"[112]

As we are reminded here, this willingness to bring our confession to God, seeking forgiveness, renewal, and healing, is to be a part of the daily rhythms of our life. But there are also times where we need to be more intentional and reflective.

Set times for self-examination may serve us well in traveling light on the journey of faith. But there may also be times where we are served well by confessing our sins to God in the presence of another person. This is so that we may hear the words of absolution and pardon.

Confession of sins is not an unhealthy focus on our weaknesses. It is an acknowledgment that we fail and need forgiveness and renewal in order to live God's life and grace.

> *Prayer: Lord, ever give me the humility of openness to your Word and Spirit so that I may be encouraged and corrected in the walk of faith and service. Amen.*

REFLECTION 112

Kindness

Gifts from an Overflowing Heart

> *But the fruit of the Spirit is love, joy, peace,*
> *patience, kindness . . .*
>
> GALATIANS 5:22

It is one thing to do things for people. It is quite another to give ourselves in love.

And those of us who come from the Western world are often so enamored with our own generosity expressed particularly in the giving of money or other resources that we become quite self-congratulatory. We think we have served others well by giving from our abundance.

Mother Teresa sees things very differently. What others need, including the poor, is first of all not simply material help. Rather, it is love. Thus, she reminds us, "Be the living expression of God's kindness: kindness in your face, kindness in your eyes, kindness in your smile, and kindness in your warm greeting."[113]

This is not sentimentalism. Nor is this a frothy spirituality. It is so much deeper. Acts of service for the poor, when done without joy and kindness, further marginalize and dehumanize them. It only deepens the poor's sense of inadequacy and failure. While the poor need bread and shelter, they also need the warmth of love. They may need our practical help, but they also need our friendship.

Kindness is the warmth of love. Kindness is the gentleness of help. Kindness is the generosity of heart that does not judge or condemn. Kindness is the depth of spirit that does not paternalize.

Kindness creates an open and free space for the other. It gives people room to move and to respond in freedom. As such, kindness is evocative. It invites a response that calls forth the best in the other, rather than a grudging acceptance of the help offered or a gratitude based in helplessness and fear.

> *Thought: While bread gives bodily sustenance, kindness covers the naked and vulnerable spirit.*

Reflection 113

God the Life-Giver

New Life As God's Gift

We were therefore buried with him through baptism into death in order that, just as Christ was raised from the dead through the glory of the Father, we too may live a new life.

ROMANS 6:4

Someone once made the comment that we should pray and trust for a person's conversion as if everything depended upon God, and we should witness and serve as if everything depended upon us.

But finally it does not depend upon us. Mother Teresa points out, "Only God can convert."[114]

This is true. Only God's Word and Spirit can penetrate our confused hearts and minds and bring light and transformation. Faith is God's gift. And to come to faith in God's work in Christ is God's mysterious doing.

Do we play a part in this? Yes, we do. It is a great privilege that God wants to use us as his witnesses. We are thus signposts pointing to Christ and to the kingdom of heaven. But there are two important ways in which we may cooperate with God's concern to bring salvation to humankind. The first is intercessory prayer. The second is faithful witness and service.

Not all people are open to hearing God's good news. And not all people are spiritually searching at a particular point in their lives. And not all people are willing to receive help. In fact, there may be a blindness and a stubborn resistance.

For such, we are invited to pray: "Lord, open their hearts. Attune them to your Spirit. Do your work of transformation, O God."

We further cooperate with God when our witness is credible. When we live in love and peace, in generosity and service to the neighbor, God may use our witness to nudge people on a spiritual quest that will bring them to the heart of God.

Prayer: Lord, at a time when so many in our world have not received your good news, may we be faithful in our witness and service, and may you, O God, pour out your Spirit upon humanity. Amen.

Doing God's Work

Living God's Call in a Needy World

To these four young men God gave knowledge and understanding of all kinds of literature and learning. And Daniel could understand visions and dreams of all kinds.

DANIEL 1:17

No one can doubt what Mother Teresa's calling was: to serve the poorest of the poor. And she saw this work as the continuation of the ministry of Jesus. She exclaims, "My heart beats in happiness; I can continue your work dear Jesus. I can ease many sorrows."[115]

Knowing what God would have us do with our lives is a great blessing. Many are not so sure. As a result, they follow careers rather than God's vocation or calling.

But it is a further blessing to know that what we are doing is a part of God's mission in our world. It is such an encouragement to know that in our work we are also serving Jesus and blessing others.

This raises the difficult question, How do I

know whether my work is continuing God's work? This can only be answered in the light of how we understand God's work in the world.

Some see this very narrowly. God's work is only the work of proclamation of the gospel. Others see this more broadly. God's work is any work that honors God, builds up the human community in love and peace, blesses others, and cares for God's creation.

It is the broader definition with the inclusion of gospel proclamation that gives us the scope of our work in the world. Thus we may be called to serve the poor, to write books, or to work in the field of economics. We may even be called to interpret dreams.

God calls his people into all the dimensions of human activity. Artist. Pastor. Politician. Banker. Missionary. But none of these spheres of activity stands independently. We work for the poor as servants of Christ. We are involved in the world of business as servants of Christ.

Reflection: It is Christ we are serving, God we are honoring, and humanity we are blessing in all we seek to do, including in our respective places of work.

REFLECTION 115

Desert Places

The Empty Spaces of the Heart

So my spirit grows faint within me; my heart within me is dismayed.

PSALM 143:4

In becoming familiar with the words and work of Mother Teresa one cannot but be impressed with the wisdom, depth of joy, and energy that pulsates through everything she does and says. Here is, indeed, a woman captivated by the love of Christ and empowered by his Spirit to do the works of love, mercy, and care.

In spite of all this, Mother Teresa also accents another theme. "There are times," she says, "when I feel absolutely empty."[116]

Energy, joy, and hope are not the only dimensions of the Christian experience. There are also times of weakness, doubt, and emptiness. We need to be particularly careful and gentle with ourselves regarding these aspects of the Christian journey. Emptiness need not be a sign of sin or difficulty. It may simply be a part of our personal psychology or an aspect of God's providential working in our lives.

High-energy people do experience times of emptiness and flatness, particularly when some important project has been completed. This is simply a part of their psychology. But it is a great providential blessing that we return to emptiness. What if it was the other way around? What if our service for God and others and the many projects we undertake would simply fill us up?

What if we would become fuller and fuller? Where would the hunger and thirst be? Where would be the seeking after God? Where would humility be?

It is in the silent and empty places that the seeking heart is found. It is in the desert places where we hunger for bread and water. It is in the acknowledgment of our need that we look for God the provider.

Emptiness is not a problem. It is, instead, a reservoir that God can fill again.

Prayer: Lord, the empty places, as much as the places filled with service and joy, are also your places. Amen.

Songs of the Heart

The Strength of Inner Joy

*May the words of my mouth and the meditation
of my heart be pleasing in your sight, O LORD, my
Rock and my Redeemer.*

PSALM 19:14

There are inner voices and there is an inner
melody that give texture to who we are and
what we do.

For some, there are the voices of negativity. So
often these come from the places of pain and disappointment. These voices hum to the discordant
tune of our inner being.

For others, there is the power of the inner
melody of joy and hope. Mother Teresa notes that
"the greatest power on earth . . . is the music of the
soul."[117] This inner harmony is a great gift because
so often we experience disharmony. We feel torn.
We are pulled in various directions at the same
time.

Both the biblical story and the history of
Christian spirituality and Christian biography
know something about this inner conflict. The

apostle Paul speaks of it in terms of not doing the good that he wants to do, or more specifically, in terms of the conflict between flesh and spirit.

The music of the soul can never be the fruit of our own efforts to achieve peace and happiness. Rather, this song of the heart comes from revelling in the grace, goodness, and generosity of God's love and forgiveness. It is a song of the redeemed soul.

What deepens the tonal texture of the melody line is the joy of living and serving and resting and giving out of a sense of doing what God wants us to do. Here obedience responds to grace and deepens the melody of the inner spirit.

What this signals to us is that the inner life is of primary importance. We may do much. We may do great things. But the strength of our life does not lie there. It lies in being at peace with God.

Meditation: Of first importance is not who we are and what we do. It is who we are before God, and who we are in his grace and through his Spirit that are of the greatest importance.

Jesus, My All

Living for Him and Because of Him

*He [Jesus] is "the stone you builders rejected,
which has become the capstone." Salvation is
found in no one else, for there is no other name
under heaven given to men by which we must be
saved.*

ACTS 4:14-15

There is no doubt that Mother Teresa loved the
poorest of the poor. She spent a good deal of
her life serving them, and she created a movement
that continues to this day to minister to the dying,
poor, lepers, abandoned children, and many others
in deep need.

There is also no doubt that Mother Teresa loved
Jesus more. In fact, her great love for the poor came
from her greater love of Jesus. Mother Teresa
makes this love clear. She comments, "To me, Jesus
is the Life I want to live, the Light I want to reflect,
the Way to the Father, the Love I want to express,
the Joy I want to share, the Peace I want to sow
around."[118]

What is striking about this confession of hers

is that she is not simply thinking of what Jesus is for her and what Jesus has done for her. Clearly, Jesus is her Life, Way, Love, Joy, and Peace. This is what Jesus has done in her. But the focus is different.

Mother Teresa is expressing an identificational theology. What she is talking about is not simply who Jesus is and what he is doing in her, but also the way in which Jesus wishes her to live toward others.

Mother Teresa sees herself joined to Christ, partaking of him, deeply embedded in his life. And as such, she sees herself living the life of Christ toward others. Thus the story of faith is not simply what Christ in his life, death, and resurrection has done on our behalf. It is also what Christ does in us and through us.

By faith we become partakers of the gift of new life that Christ gives us. But we also become joined to him and to his redemptive and healing purposes for our world.

Thought: The imitation of Christ can only come about by being in Christ by the power of the Holy Spirit.

REFLECTION 118

Sacrifice

The Heart of the Mystery of Faith

*For all have sinned and fall short of the glory of
God and are justified freely by his grace through
the redemption that came by Christ Jesus. God
presented him as a sacrifice of atonement,
through faith in his blood.*

ROMANS 3:23-25

In the daily realities of life we know something
about sacrifice. Parents make sacrifices to better the opportunities for their children. One may
make sacrifices to help a friend.

But generally speaking, in contemporary
Western culture at least, the idea of sacrifice is
unpopular. We want much, and we want what is
best for us. And even Western aid to the Two-thirds
World is hardly sacrificial.

However, sacrifice does lie at the heart of the
Christian faith and experience. In the Old Testa-
ment, sacrifices were central to the religious cult.
Sin against purity required sacrifice. And in the New
Testament, Jesus becomes the sin bearer who takes
upon himself the shame and guilt of the world.

So at the heart of the Christian faith we confess that God gave his Son as a sacrifice so that we could experience new life through reconciliation, forgiveness, and healing. What is astounding is the reversal. It is not that a just God demands a sacrifice from us. It is a just God providing a sacrifice on our behalf. This is the story of grace.

The Christian life brought to birth by sacrifice calls for sacrifice. This is not sacrifice to achieve reconciliation. It is sacrifice that comes from having been forgiven. It is the sacrifice of gratitude.

Mother Teresa is, therefore, right: "Sacrifice is at the heart of Christian faith."[119] And the sacrifice of gratitude is living a life that seeks to please and honor God and bless others.

Mother Teresa lived sacrificially to serve the poorest of the poor. We are called to live in similar ways wherever God has called us. One can be a top businessperson and still live sacrificially for the sake of Christ and the gospel.

> *Reflection*: What sacrifices do I need to continue to bring to God in living a life of fidelity and obedience?

REFLECTION 119

Fullness

Filled with God's Spirit

Therefore do not be foolish, but understand what the Lord's will is. Do not get drunk on wine, which leads to debauchery. Instead, be filled with the Spirit.

EPHESIANS 5:17-18

One of the sad misconceptions of the Western mind-set is the idea that we can have everything. We have much in material possessions *and* can be happy as well. We can have our individualism *and* experience community as well. We can have our Western values *and* have God as well. We can live for ourselves *and* be spiritual as well.

But things don't work that way in God's economy. God's ways are different. They are often paradoxical. And Mother Teresa points to this when she remarks, "God cannot fill what is full, he can only fill emptiness."[120]

We don't come easily to the place of emptiness because we readily think that fullness is our right, or at least our expectation. It is usually trials or difficulties that bring us to the place of openness and receptivity.

If we are too full of our own importance, we can hardly be full of the fruit of the Spirit. If we are too full of our own abilities, we can hardly be full of the power of the Spirit. And when we are too full of our own prayers, we cannot expect the Spirit to be praying through us.

Moreover, our lives can be too full of Christian service! As a consequence, our lives are not full of the presence of God because God has been pushed to the periphery of our busy lives.

Again and again, we have to stop in our tracks and realize anew that we are to live in and for God. And in humility we have to acknowledge that we need God to be our life, strength, and joy.

To be full of God's Spirit is not the fruit of a momentary surrender. It is, instead, the outflow of a life of friendship and fellowship with the God who sustains us.

Meditation: Where are the places in life where I am too full? And where do I need to become empty so that I may truly be filled?

Temptation

Resisting Turning Back

On reaching the place, he said to them, "Pray that you will not fall into temptation."

LUKE 22:40

No one is outside the realm of testing and temptation. And the temptation to turn back occurs frequently when someone has made a costly commitment to follow and serve God in a particular way.

Mother Teresa also experienced this when unsuccessfully looking for a center in which to conduct her ministry to the poorest of the poor. She comments, "Then the comfort of Loreto came to tempt me."[121]

One of the most basic lessons of the spiritual life that we need to learn again and again is that obedience to God's will does not mean that everything will go smoothly and easily. In fact, the opposite may well be the case. The road is rocky and difficult, and so we think about turning back.

The reason why this is so difficult for us is that

on the road of obedience we expect that God will protect us and provide for us, just as he provided for his people in the long and terrible journey through the desert to the Promised Land.

The surprise is that God does provide, as he did for his people Israel and for Mother Teresa, and also for you. But God does not provide when and how we expect. In God's sovereignty and providence, God's provision so often comes when we have resisted the temptation to give up or to turn back.

In this, we receive a double blessing—both the things that we desired for the service of God, and a deepening of our faith and resolve to trust God's way even when our hands are empty.

In doing God's work, his provision will come, but seldom in the way we expect. This is the way of humility we are called to walk.

Prayer: Lord, when you have shown me the way, help me to walk faithfully in your footsteps, not doubting your protection, care, and provision. Amen.

The Word of God

Knowing, Living, Sharing the Gospel

When Jesus had called the Twelve together, he gave them power and authority to drive out all demons and to cure diseases, and he sent them out to preach the kingdom of God and to heal the sick.

LUKE 9:1-2

Mother Teresa, with disarming simplicity, speaks of a crucial dimension in living the Christian life. She notes, "Know the Word of God [and] love . . . live . . . give the Word of God."[122]

This order is important. One cannot live and give what one does not know. To know is where it all begins. And knowing the Word of God is not simply an intellectual knowing, but also a knowing of the heart. It is God's Word finding a resting place within our very being.

When God's Word not only enlightens us, but also sustains us and directs us, then we may say that we are beginning to live the Word of God. The Word of God becomes our spiritual food and the light that guides us.

But good things are to be shared. And the good gifts of God are for the people of God and for all humanity. The Word of God is to be hidden in our hearts and shared with friends and strangers alike. Being a Christian is being a gossiper of the gospel.

But the Word of God is a Word that is not merely suggestive. It is also transformative. It is a Word that sets people free. It is a Word that brings healing.

By the Word, God made the heavens and the earth. By his Word of covenant, he called his Old Testament people into being. And in Christ, the Living Word, God has revealed his salvation and his healing and renewing power.

The Word of God is powerful good news. And those who know this Word and live by it may proclaim this Word as a Word that makes all things new.

Thought: To live the Word of God is to be renewed by it, and to proclaim the Word of God is to see others transformed by it.

Spiritual Pruning

Submitting to God's Work of Transformation

He cuts off every branch in me that bears no fruit,
while every branch that does bear fruit he prunes
so that it will be even more fruitful.

JOHN 15:2

Much of contemporary Christianity is marked by activism, but not by spiritual wisdom. And many of the values of capitalism have been dragged into our understanding of the way God works in the world. Thus we believe that Christian activity will always be productive. Moreover, we are always thinking about expanding our ministries.

At the individual level we tend to think the same. In Christian growth we will become happier, stronger, and more blessed.

But a counter voice needs to be raised. Not only is the above not an adequate picture, it is not a good picture either. It is too optimistic and linear and monochrome. It is a picture without light and shadows.

The gospel speaks about a pruning process in

the midst of fruitfulness that leaves us naked and bare. And Mother Teresa echoes these sentiments. She comments, "You must allow the Father to be a gardener, to prune. You will be pruned, don't worry."[123]

What we fail to accent in contemporary Christianity is that not only are things given to us, but things are also taken away. This is the pruning process. What is taken away from us is not simply the bad, but also the good. And for this, we are not well prepared. We think that with good, God will give more good. But God may well take things from us: our ministry, our health, our resources.

Awesome are the pruning shears in the hand of God. And we are left exposed and vulnerable.

While this will most likely drive us to unhealthy introspection and blame finding or to self-pity and complaint, we will need to learn to love the very hand that seemingly wounds us.

Meditation: The heavy hand of God will grant us lightness of being.

Revealed and Hidden

The Double Movement of Contemplation

> *And is not the bread that we break a participation in the body of Christ? Because there is one loaf, we, who are many, are one body, for we all partake of the one loaf.*
>
> 1 CORINTHIANS 10:16-17

The New Testament writers see a connection between the Lord's Supper or Eucharist and the church as the body of Christ. The community of faith is nourished by the Eucharist, but the Eucharist also acts as a metaphor symbolizing the unity and love in the church.

As an extension of this idea, Christians are called to love and serve Christ, but they are also called to love and serve one another as members of the body of Christ, the church. And serving members of the body of Christ is one way to serve Christ himself.

Mother Teresa takes this idea one step further. She notes, "The Christ who gives of himself to us under the appearance of bread and the Christ who is hidden under the distressing disguise of the poor, is the same Jesus."[124] This means that not only is serving the brothers and sisters in the community of faith a way of serving Christ, but in serving the poor we are serving Christ in hidden and disfigured form.

For Mother Teresa this forms the spiritual motivation for service to the poorest of the poor. This brings contemplation and service together. In worship one meets the revealed Christ. In service to the poor one meets the hidden Christ.

Her basis for this position is Matthew 25:40 where Jesus said, "Whatever you did for one of the least of these . . . you did for me."

This double movement of contemplation and action makes service a form of worship. Or to put that differently, this infuses service with a profound spirituality. For in serving the poor one is serving Christ himself.

> *Meditation: I can see Christ clearly in Word and sacrament, and even in the church, the body of Christ. Can I also see Christ in my family, the neighbor, the stranger, and even my enemy?*

A Difficult Obedience

The Hard Tasks That Are Part of Our Calling

I may not be a trained speaker, but I do have knowledge.

2 CORINTHIANS 11:6

Paul saw himself as an apostle of Jesus Christ and lived his life accordingly. But there were difficult things he had to contend with, including trouble in the churches dealing with accusations from those Paul called false apostles. There were many dimensions to Paul's apostolic task that he would have found difficult and cumbersome.

It was similar for Mother Teresa. She comments, "I am requested to speak in public. This is an ordeal for me."[125] It is clear that Mother Teresa found great joy in serving the poor and training her sisters. But public speaking was a heavy burden that she nevertheless fulfilled for the sake of the ministry.

And so it is with us. Whether we are working out our calling in the family, the neighborhood, service in the church, or work in the marketplace, there are aspects of the overall task that we find difficult. And yet they need to be done.

This calls for a spiritual obedience for which we need to find special grace. It also highlights our limitations. We cannot do everything well — everything is not a reflection of our giftedness, and so there are tasks that need to be done that weigh heavily upon us.

The challenge for us is not to resign ourselves to these realities, but to see them as opportunities for growth. We don't always need to be within our comfort zones. To be pushed beyond our normal boundaries provides us with opportunities to trust God more fully for his grace and empowerment.

Even what we find difficult to do can be brought to God as an act of service and worship.

> *Reflection:* What do I do with the tasks I
> find difficult? Avoid? Engage? Tolerate?
> Embrace?

Confessing Christ

Christ As Center and Purpose
for All I Do

*For in Christ all the fullness of the Deity lives in
bodily form, and you have been given fullness in
Christ, who is the head over every power and
authority.*

COLOSSIANS 2:9-10

There are healthy generality and particularity
that run through the sayings and speeches of
Mother Teresa. On the one hand, she can say that
we are all God's children whether we are Hindu,
Muslim, or Christian. Here she means that we are
all made in God's image and are the objects of God's
love.

On the other hand, she also recognizes that
there are many religions with their different ways
of seeking God. And here she is very particular
about her position. "I follow Christ," she says. And
she goes on to confess, "Jesus is my God . . .
Spouse . . . Life . . . Love . . . All in All."[126] It is
evident that Mother Teresa not only believed this,
but lived this as well. Christ was her very life, not

only her faith.

This is a challenge for us as we live in increasingly multicultural contexts. We can recognize the importance of other religions but live our own faith with a greater fidelity and integrity. In fact, if we don't live this way we will become lost in a world of generalities.

In a multicultural and multireligious world, we cannot live our faith in Christ with a greater tolerance and ease. Surprisingly, the opposite is called for. We are challenged to live in Christ more fully, more prayerfully, and with greater service and witness.

In a tolerant world we will either become comfortable compromisers or we will live the gospel with greater attentiveness. A tolerant world needs to see saints, martyrs, and radicals in order that the light of Christ may shine more fully.

Meditation: What does Christ, as my all, look like in my life of work and service?

REFLECTION 126

Suffering

Hearing Its Call to Come to the Heart of God

Now if we are children, then we are heirs—heirs of God and coheirs with Christ, if indeed we share in his sufferings, in order that we may also share in his glory.

ROMANS 8:17

In the First World, suffering has become very problematical. We believe that it is unfair and unnecessary. And we will do anything we can to avoid or negate suffering.

In the Two-thirds World, the attitude toward suffering is different. It is seen as integral to life and, therefore, cannot be avoided. It can only be embraced.

Mother Teresa has this to say about suffering: "It is not a punishment. Jesus does not punish. Suffering is a sign—that we have come so close to Jesus on the cross."[127]

Suffering is a part of life. It is a reflection of the fallenness of our world. This suffering can come to us in general ways in that we all may be impacted by a natural disaster or by some other tragedy that affects our community.

But suffering can also touch us in more specific and personal ways: a sickness in the family, loss of a loved one, family abuse, loss of a job. Loss can take many forms and suffering has many tones and textures.

Some forms of suffering are a wake-up call. They are reminders that we are called to a greater fidelity. Other forms of suffering have the value of drawing us closer to God. They help us in identifying more closely with the suffering God, the Christ on the cross.

Our own suffering can assist us in entering more fully into the sufferings of God who wills his *shalom* to come to all the earth, yet allows humans to make choices for peace or war, for greed or generosity, for selfishness or justice.

Thought: In what ways can the suffering in my life be redemptive?

REFLECTION 127

A Greater Vision

Seeing the Present in the Light of Eternity

Then the King will say to those on his right, "Come, you who are blessed by my Father; take your inheritance, the kingdom prepared for you since the creation of the world."

MATTHEW 25:34

Mother Teresa regularly prayed this prayer: "Come, O blessed Spirit of knowledge and light, and grant that I may perceive the will of the Father. Show me the nothingness of earthly things, that I may realize their vanity and use them only for your glory . . . looking ever beyond them to you in your eternal reward."[128]

We, too, could pray this prayer again and again, for here we find a set of themes that are key to the Christian life.

Our life with God is dependent on the work of the Holy Spirit. The Spirit is the great Revealer. The Spirit opens the dark places with penetrating light. The Spirit broods within us, ever drawing us more deeply into the life of God.

The Spirit has a particular intentionality. The Spirit wants us to participate, not only in the life of God, but also in the purposes of God. The Spirit wishes to guide us in such a way that our lives become the instruments that God can use for his purposes.

In hearing and knowing the will of God, we need to resist becoming enamored with the values and idolatries of our world. While we wish to see the world as God's good gift and while we recognize that God has given the gifts of his creation for our benefit and blessing, we also recognize that there are emphases in our culture that take us away from God's kingdom purposes. Thus in knowing the will of God we say yes to God's purposes and no to the worldliness of the world.

The willingness to say no to aspects of what is offered to us in this life requires both the empowerment of the Spirit and an eschatological vision. In the light of God's final picture of new heavens and a new earth, we see that there are things here that do not matter and therefore we can let them go.

Thought: Adopt or create a prayer that is comprehensive enough to be your prayer for days and even months or years.

Receiving and Giving

The Double Movement of the Christian Life

*Ask and it will be given to you. . . . If you,
then, though you are evil, know how to give good gifts
to your children, how much more will your
Father in heaven give good gifts to those who ask
him!*

MATTHEW 7:7,11

Central to the Christian life is the joyous experience of receiving. We are invited to receive from God, in Christ, the blessings of salvation: reconciliation, forgiveness, healing, and empowerment.

We never receive these blessings without the invitation to open our hearts and hands more fully so that we may be the glad recipients of all that God wishes to give us. Thus Mother Teresa counsels us, "The more we receive in silent prayer, the more we can give in our active life."[129]

There are many ways in which we can apply this key idea of a double movement of receiving and giving. The more we live in God's presence, the more we can carry the presence of God to others. The more we live in the love of God, the more we can express that love to family, colleagues, and neighbors.

Thus we need to be careful that our giving does not exceed our receiving. What I mean is that we cannot give what we do not have, and we cannot give well when we are discouraged.

This ongoing receptivity calls us to a great humility. We think we can do much. We think we can keep giving. We think we can keep on going. But so often we have to scale back. We have to realize our limitations. We have to stop, to pray, to reflect, to receive.

Put more basically, great and consistent giving calls for deep rest, true Sabbath, and Spirit empowerment. There is no virtue in an orgy of giving and a life of burnout. A life of receiving is a life that is truly sustained.

And while good giving has many challenges, receiving also has its own wisdom. It requires time rather than haste, surprise rather than predictability, the open hand rather than the closed heart.

Thought: Being open to what God wants to give will always be a greater challenge than what we want to give to others.

Accepting Limitations

Human Need and God's Provision

*And do not forget to do good and to share with
others, for with such sacrifices God is pleased.*
HEBREWS 13:16

Mother Teresa makes a simple acknowledgment: "The needs are always greater than our
ability to meet them."[130] She is referring to her work
among the poorest of the poor, including lepers
and abandoned children.

But this is true more broadly. At every level of
life, needs outstrip resources. We need more love
in our homes, better healthcare in our medical
services, and greater wholeness in our churches.
The burning question is how do we respond to
this? What do we do with human limitations? How
do we process the fact that blatant problems continue in our world?

One unacceptable response is sheer denial!
There are still people who say that things are
okay. These people look at the world from the
position of their relative well-being and judge
less fortunate people as being lazy and respon-

sible for their own misfortunes.

Another equally unacceptable response is that of passive resignation. One frequently hears people lament human need and the problems of our world, but claim that nothing can be done because the problems are simply too big.

A third response is at the opposite end of the previous perspective. This is the position of a blinded optimist who holds that we can fix things if only we try a little harder and act a little fairer. But this is naive. The problems of our lives and world go much deeper than that.

A more biblical response looks quite different. This recognizes the goodness of God in providing for this world. But it also recognizes the human realities of sin, greed, and exploitation. These sad truths about ourselves invite us to come to God for forgiveness and inner renewal. And out of this ongoing transformation of our lives we are called to care for, proclaim good news to, and advocate on behalf of those who are needy.

Reflection: Human need invites us to wash the feet of the world.

Dejected

Facing Our Discouragements

Why are you downcast, O my soul? Why so disturbed within me? Put your hope in God, for I will yet praise him, my Savior and my God.

PSALM 42:5-6

We need to be very careful and gentle with ourselves and others when we or they are experiencing discouragement. It is especially important that we don't confuse clinical depression with the more general feelings of dejection. The former condition requires professional help. The latter requires general sensitivity, care, and encouragement.

Mother Teresa's gentle reminder is, "Do not ever allow sadness to take such a hold of your spirit that it leads you to forget the joy of the resurrected Christ."[131] I wish to add some further perspectives to this insight.

Feeling discouragement and dejection is normal to life. It is also normal to the Christian experience. Not only does life bring its disappointments and setbacks, so does Christian ministry and service. In fact, Christian service may at times be particularly discouraging. We so much want to see people blessed, and yet change and transformation is often such a slow journey.

It is important in times of discouragement that we don't fall into the doubtful art of blaming. We blame others for not responding. Or we blame ourselves for not being sufficiently effective.

Times of discouragement invite us to bring our disconsolate selves to God. They invite us to bring God into our discouragement. *Lord, we had hoped for much and yet so little has happened. Lord, the people I thought would help have let me down. Lord, we have put so much energy into this project yet nothing seems to be going well.*

So Lord, I am handing these matters over to you. I need the gift of hope and perseverance. I need the blessing of joy in the midst of adversity. And I need your grace to continue to live and serve in faith, hope, and love.

>   **Reflection:** I need grace for the whole jour-
>   ney, not only for the enthusiastic beginnings
>   and for the good parts, but for the difficult
>   terrain as well.

REFLECTION 131

Love

Beyond Conditional Service

Dear friends, since God so loved us, we also
ought to love one another. No one has ever seen
God; but if we love one another, God lives in us
and his love is made complete in us.

1 JOHN 4:11-12

L ove is probably the most sentimentalized
word in our contemporary culture. But in the
biblical story love is about self-giving. Mother
Teresa is, therefore, right when she emphasizes that
"the fruit of love is service."[132]

To love another person is to value and know
that person. Moreover, this valuing expresses
itself in attention, availability, nurture, and care.
Or to put it differently, love expresses itself in acts
of kindness and service.

For the Christian, love is to take on some further dimensions. This love that we have been
speaking about is not only for family and friends.
It is also to be extended to the stranger, and even
to the enemy.

It is particularly at this point that we recognize

how far we fall short of this vision of love. It is at this point that we see how much the love of God still needs to penetrate our being. The love of Christ was a love that served. It was a love by which Christ was willing to give his life. It was a love by which he forgave his enemies, those who crucified him.

A Christian is a person who has been marked by the love of Christ. The Christian life, therefore, is cruciform. It is marked by the cross. But instead of the cross being a sign of despair and senseless cruelty, it is a sign of hope, a sign of love. To love is to be in God. To love is to be like God. And to love is to live and serve in the way that Christ did.

True service cannot come out of pity or out of control. It can only come from a love that has the well-being of the other in view.

Meditation: Christ loved us. Can we grow in that love so that this is the love that we extend to others?

Certainty

Hearing God's Call

*But the LORD took me from tending the flock and
said to me, "Go, prophesy to my people Israel."*
AMOS 7:15

We live in a world of great uncertainties. We
have no control over our health and well-
being, although we can live carefully. And we have
no control over what happens politically and eco-
nomically in our world, although we can make
personal choices and commitments that foster
peace and prosperity.

The personal and spiritual dimensions of our
lives are also marked by uncertainty. There are
times when God seems absent. We may experience
crises of faith.

So are there things we can be sure about in the
journey of faith? The answer to this is a clear yes.
But the yes has a certain texture. Our certainty is
not the same as a scientific certainty, such as the
law of gravity. It is different. It will always be a certainty of faith.

Mother Teresa was sure of her call to serve the

poorest of the poor. She comments, "I was sure it was God's voice. I was certain he was calling me."[133]

This is a certainty of faith. There were no "objective" indicators and guarantees. But her subsequent journey of serving the poor, young people joining her order, financial provision, and the evident power of the witness of this work for God are indicators that God had indeed called her.

And so it is with the many dimensions of the Christian life. We trust the God who has revealed himself to us. We imbibe his Word and promises. We experience the presence and guidance of the Holy Spirit. We are nurtured within the community of faith through worship, teaching, sacraments, fellowship, and service.

All of this is the tapestry of certainty. Personally and communally we experience God's presence and goodness. And even the times of doubt and God's seeming absence are not enough to erode the membranes of faith and trust.

> *Reflection: There are the signs of God in the world he has made. There are the promises of God in the Word he has spoken. There is the evidence of God's love in the Son he has given. There is the power of the presence of God in the Spirit poured out upon us.*

All Things Possible

*Journeying with the God
of the Impossible*

*He who did not spare his own Son, but gave him
up for us all—how will he not also, along with
him, graciously give us all things?*

ROMANS 8:32

It is appropriate to emphasize the uncertainty and vulnerability of life in the world. But it is equally appropriate to confess the trustworthiness and generosity of God.

What is particularly appropriate is to acknowledge and celebrate that the God of the Bible is the One who will also provide for us. This provision is never dependent on our spirituality or piety. It is based on the generous nature of God himself.

However, there is another side to this story. We will be all the more confident of God's care and provision when we are seeking these blessings, not simply for ourselves, but also on behalf of others.

Mother Teresa expresses this beautifully. She points out, "Persuaded of our nothingness and with the blessing of obedience we attempt all things, doubting nothing, for with God all things are possible."[134]

In the stories of the Missionaries of Charity, there are many examples of God's provision: food brought to one of their homes when the cupboards were bare; access into closed access countries; the sudden cessation of bombing to allow the sisters to enter an area of civil unrest and conflict. These stories can be multiplied.

What is at work here is the mysterious synchronicity between faith and prayer and the providential care of God. God provides when we pray and call out to him. And we do this with confidence particularly when this is not for our own benefit but has to do with blessing others.

To serve God's redemptive and healing purposes in our world as the servants of Christ puts us in a place where we can trust God to care for us and to provide for us, particularly in the good things we seek to extend to others in Christ's name.

> *Thought: The more the kingdom of God is central to who we are and what we do, the more we can trust that the blessings of the kingdom will be poured out on us and on those we seek to serve.*

By Deeds

Incarnating the Gospel

*Live such good lives among the pagans that,
though they accuse you of doing wrong, they may
see your good deeds and glorify God on the day
he visits us.*

1 PETER 2:12

There are many ways of being a faithful witness and servant of Christ. We can be this in prayer, in proclamation, and in service. And we are called to be the servants of Christ in our homes, churches, neighborhoods, schools, and places of work.

Being a witness for Christ is particularly challenging in our kind of world. Not only are we living in a post-Christendom era, but people are quite cynical about many institutions, including the church.

Mother Teresa is quite convinced that service is a powerful form of witness. She prays, "Let us preach you without preaching, not by words, but by our example."[135]

Mother Teresa believes that love in action not

only gives us the opportunity to help and bless the other person, but that this also opens the way for the sharing of the good news of the gospel. The deeds of the gospel make way for the words of the gospel.

All of this is not to say that deeds are to have a priority over words. But words that speak of love must find their expression in deeds that reflect love.

God loves and gives us the gift of his Son. Jesus loves and gives us the gift of his life. The Spirit loves and gives us the blessings of charisms.

And so we love because we are loved and we have been given so much. We love and serve from the free place of thankfulness and joy. We wish to bless because we are blessed.

And in our service, we can find no greater joy than that others find the source of love and joy that animates us. We rejoice when others find the gift of life in Christ by the Holy Spirit.

> *Meditation: If deeds are windows into the heart of the action, how can my deeds of love be windows into the heart of God?*

Christian Community

The Practice of Togetherness

*All the believers were together and had every-
thing in common.*

ACTS 2:44

It is very easy to misread the Mother Teresa story.
One can so readily focus on her service to the
poorest of the poor that one loses from view the
profound spirituality that infused her life and her
order.

What can also be lost from view is that while
service is important, building community is
equally important. Put differently, service to the
poor is a communal ministry and is sustained by
life in community.

Mother Teresa comments, "Our first great
responsibility is to be a family, a community,
revealing first to one another something of God's
own love and concern and tenderness."[136]

This is an important challenge to the way in
which we "do church," particularly in the Western
world. Here church is basically an institution. And
we come to church to participate in religious activ-

ities. And the church provides religious services. We generally don't see church as family and as community.

Yet in many ways that is precisely what church is meant to be. It is the body of Christ, the family of God, the community of faith. And the church's self-understanding should be that we are a fellowship of brothers and sisters in Christ.

Such a fellowship is created around a key vision, namely, that just as Christ laid down his life for us in service and sacrifice, so we should love and serve one another.

Mother Teresa is, therefore, right. Our life should be rooted in God and in community. And the blessings and richness that we receive there can be carried over in service to the neighbor. This is to be as true of the church as it is of the Missionaries of Charity.

> *Thought: Building life together is also building life that will bless us and will empower us for costly service.*

REFLECTION 136

The Christ

Living the Imitatio Christi

For in Christ all the fullness of the Deity lives in bodily form, and you have been given fullness in Christ, who is the head over every power and authority.

COLOSSIANS 2:9-10

Mother Teresa, in making one of her most profound yet simple statements, gets to the heart of what life and service and witness are all about. She exclaims, "Jesus explains our life."[137]

There is a great depth to this statement and there are many ways in which it could be interpreted. There are two basic ways in which I wish to engage this key phrase.

The first is that the life, death, and resurrection of Christ are God's most profound ways of responding to the human condition. In Christ is found the solution to human alienation and sin. In him is found the way of reconciliation, forgiveness, healing, and peace. In this sense, Christ explains our life — our life as problem and our life as need. In other words, Christ is the way for us.

In him are found the answers for our guilt, confusion, and waywardness.

There is also a second way to engage this phrase. Christ explains our life in the sense that Christ becomes normative for us. The way Christ lived, loved, and served is the way in which we are called to love and serve.

Here we are speaking about discipleship, obedient following, and the *imitatio Christi*. Redeemed by Christ, we seek to be like him. And being like him involves following Christ in his passion, service, and love.

Thus we, too, seek to be servants rather than masters. We, too, seek to bring reconciliation and peace. We, too, seek to serve the poor.

All of this means that Christ is central to the way we live. He is, indeed, our Lord. And nothing gives us greater joy than to see others blessed by the Christ who gave his life for the world.

Reflection: The true nature of what life is all about is clearly displayed in the person and work of Christ.

The Church Militant and Triumphant

A Humble and Grand Vision of the People of God

*So that you may become blameless and pure,
children of God without fault in a crooked and
depraved generation, in which you shine like
stars in the universe.*

PHILIPPIANS 2:15

There are many ways of thinking about being the people of God, the body of Christ. One way is to think about the church sociologically, as a religious institution. Another is to think about the community of faith as a theological reality, people who by faith are linked to Christ and made one by the power of the Spirit. A further way is to think about the church eschatologically, the people of God throughout history who also will one day celebrate the marriage supper of the Lamb of God.

Mother Teresa had no small vision. She explains, "I want to have a Glorious Society in heaven, the Suffering Society on earth . . . [and] the

Militant Society—the sisters in the battlefield."[138] In this, she saw those in heaven cheering us on, those suffering offering prayers, and those serving the poor as being the agents of love, care, and transformation.

This is a grand vision and one that cuts across the narrow individualism that so often characterizes those who seek to do the more difficult acts of Christian service. So often they see themselves as the solo heroes of the faith. But the works of God cannot be done by the few, only by the many. And the many needs require the prayers of many.

This grander vision links prophets and activists with contemplatives and intercessors. It links pastors with those in the marketplace. It links the church on earth with the church in heaven.

God's work is the task of the whole people of God. And all are called and invited to play a role. Some give. Some serve. Some heal. Some pray. Some prophesy. Some set up businesses. Some empower the poor.

> *Meditation: Christ is the Lord of history, of the present, and of the coming kingdom. In serving Christ the Lord, we become linked to the long trail of the faithful, the present-serving church of faith, and the church of God's final kingdom.*

First Things First

Serving the Whole Person

*He went to him and bandaged his wounds,
pouring on oil and wine. Then he put the man on
his donkey, took him to an inn and took care of
him.*

LUKE 10:34

The gospel invites us to love the other by caring for him or her. And our care should be expressed by responding to the most immediate and pressing needs.

To put this differently, while we may want to respond first to the spiritual needs of a person, because we see this as most fundamental and important, that may not at all be appropriate. This is particularly so if the person does not acknowledge such a need and if other needs are more pressing—namely, the person is suffering from serious malnutrition.

Mother Teresa is very clear about this matter. She comments, "We must first satisfy the needs of the body, so we can bring Christ to the poor."[139]

This central idea has many applications to the

way in which we seek to respond to others. Most basically, it challenges us to rethink whether our response to others is based on what *we* think they need or whether it is based on what the other person is needing and asking for.

We need to recognize that so often we are agenda-driven in what we seek to do for others. As a result, *we* are at the center and not the person we are helping. This means our helping is all about *us* and not them.

But if we truly love and seek to serve, the other person must be most fully in view. Consequently, we may first need to befriend rather than help. We may first need to listen rather than advise. We may first need to feed rather than counsel.

So often, the works of the gospel must precede the words of the gospel. The deeds of love must precede the words of love. Deeds must precede proclamation.

Thought: Do what needs to be done and trust God to provide the opening for witness and sharing.

A Double Conversion

Rich and Poor Need Each Other

*But Zacchaeus stood up and said to the Lord,
"Look, Lord! Here and now I give half of my possessions to the poor, and if I have cheated anyone
out of anything, I will pay back four times the
amount."*

LUKE 19:8

The good news of Christ is for all, both rich and
poor alike. And God's salvation is for all, for
all are sinners and fall short of God's glory and
holiness.

While both rich and poor need God's grace and
forgiveness, their respective social situations and
circumstances of life are very different. The one
group has power, status, and resources. The other
is powerless, marginalized, and in deep need.

The big surprise in God's kingdom purposes is
that *both* need each other. We would expect this
to be different—that the poor need the rich. But
the rich need the poor as well.

Mother Teresa knows this mystery of the
kingdom of God. She notes, "What we desire is not

a class struggle but a class encounter, in which the rich save the poor and the poor save the rich."[140]

How might this be? we may very well ask. And how can the poor help the rich?

In coming to Christ in faith and trust, we become followers of Christ, and this becomes the more central reality of who we are—not the fact that we are rich or poor, black or white, male or female. And as disciples of Christ, we are called to share what we have with those within the community of faith.

Sharing, however, is a two-way street. The rich may share out of their abundance of resources; the poor may share their vulnerability and hope. The rich may share their strength; the poor may give of their brokenness. The rich may only know about the powerful Christ; the poor may teach them about the suffering Christ.

So often we can learn from the poor that happiness lies not in much-having. Moreover, the poor can teach us about resilience in the face of difficulty and hope in the face of despair.

> *Reflection: The rich need the poor as much as the other way around, for in the poor the rich can hear the voice of God calling them to generosity and humanity.*

In God's Hands

Held by the Firmness of God's Love

*Can a mother forget the baby at her breast and
have no compassion on the child she has borne?
Though she may forget, I will not forget you! See,
I have engraved you on the palms of my hands.*
ISAIAH 49:15-16

In the face of the eventuality of death, we are most vulnerable and powerless. But in many other ways we are vulnerable as well. We are affected by the tyrannies of our world and by the fragility of our personal relationships.

And so we may well ask, Where is the place of safety and security? Where can I be sheltered and protected?

Mother Teresa provides a most basic answer. "God looks at the palms of his hands and sees us there."[141] In this powerful metaphor we see the heartbeat of God. Not only are we held in God's hands of protection, nurture, and care, but we are held in the scarred hands of God in Christ.

This means that there is nothing cheap and easy about God's care and love. To be in God's hands is to be in suffering hands that know the pain of hatred and rejection. But they are, in spite of this, the hands of forgiveness and embrace. The scarred hands are healing hands. In being held by God's love we are not only protected, but we're also made whole.

The Christian life, therefore, is never first of all about clinging to God, but being held by God. The most profound mystery is that God knows me! Known and loved by God, who in Christ gave his life for me, I am known, loved, and secure.

This security is an eternal one in time. It is the security of faith. This security of the Spirit is God being present with us now.

Thought: Held fast. Being held. Held in love and care. Held in the now. Held forever.

REFLECTION 141

Work

Beyond Duty and Obligation

*God is not unjust; he will not forget your work
and the love you have shown him as you have
helped his people and continue to help them.*
HEBREWS 6:10

There are many kinds of work. There is paid
employment. There is housework. We also do
voluntary work. And there is the work of Christian
service.

These different kinds of activities all have
their particular challenges. In some there are the
challenges of long hours. In others there is the
sense of drudgery. And in Christian service there
is often the sense that while much is hoped for, so
little seems to change.

The kind of work we do is not the only issue.
But the attitude that we bring to our work is also
important. Work done out of mere necessity will
hardly be as meaningful as the work of creativity.

At this point Mother Teresa's perceptive comment is helpful. She comments, "Work without
love is slavery."[142]

While this is particularly true among the poorest of the poor, it is true of all work whether it be paid employment, housework, or Christian service. We need constantly to remind ourselves that there is no such thing as mere work. Work has some purpose and it is an expression of who we are and what we value. Moreover, work has some ultimate purpose. In work we seek to glorify God, build his church, and contribute to the human condition, and as such, we seek to do good in our world.

Work can easily become a burden. And we can easily begin to work grudgingly. Thus, there is no joy in what we do.

Work marked by joy and care, on the other hand, is work that will bless others and will sustain us. Thus our work must come from spirituality. It must spring from the wellspring of the generous and serving heart fed by the fountain of God.

Reflection: Love is the expression of the generous heart. This love may sculpt all that I do, including my work.

REFLECTION 142

Human Finitude

Acknowledging the Human Condition

> *Come, let us bow down in worship, let us kneel*
> *before the LORD our Maker.*
>
> PSALM 95:6

It usually doesn't take too much success before we begin to think of ourselves as somewhat larger than life and as better than others. Pride is, after all, a primal sin with a contemporary sting.

While pride may stalk the halls of the academy, the machinations of politics, and the boardrooms of the multinationals, it also plagues the sanctuary. And spiritual pride is probably the greatest affront to the mystery of the Incarnation where the weak and the least are welcomed to God's banqueting table.

The problem with pride is the blinding effect it has on the one who thinks he or she is so good or so strong. And while the blind stumble, God wants us to walk in the light.

Mother Teresa points us in a totally different direction. "Self knowledge," she observes, "puts us on our knees."[143]

If we truly know ourselves, we will acknowledge that we are mere creatures capable of much good, but also marred by failure and sin. Moreover, we will have to admit that whatever we have achieved has been as much the contribution of others as it has been the fruit of our own labor.

But even more basically, true self-knowledge yields the cry of the wounded heart and the needy life. No matter how much we have in terms of material possessions, there is in all of us the hunger for love and meaning.

In the final analysis, we are the restless seekers for the God who welcomes home those who realize that the presence of God is our final home, that grace is the final gift, and that worship is the final act.

Thus, to be on our knees before our Maker is not an act of humiliation. It is a posture of humility.

Meditation: Pride is exploded by the gentle grace of humility.

Meet the Master

Celebrating the Great Guest

Philip found Nathanael and told him, "We have found the one Moses wrote about in the Law, and about whom the prophets also wrote—Jesus of Nazareth, the son of Joseph." "Nazareth! Can anything good come from there?" Nathanael asked. "Come and see," said Philip.

JOHN 1:45-46

Mother Teresa developed a regular practice of taking people who came to visit her first to the chapel. It mattered not that some of these people were the most rich, famous, and powerful people in the world.

She comments, "Whenever a visitor comes to this house, I take him [or her] to the chapel for a while. I tell him [or her], 'Let us first greet the Master of the house.'"[144]

This custom is simplicity at its most profound level. For this is not only a form of witness to Christ, it is more basically a reflection of a whole way of life. It says Christ is central. Christ is Lord.

The repetition of this by way of application to

the world of business and commerce, or that of industry and manufacture, is not simply that Christian owners should have chapels in the workplace, even though that may be a good idea. Rather, something much more basic should play itself out here.

That something is celebrating the lordship of Christ in the places where we find ourselves, whether that be home, school, work, or play. It is living the great truth that nothing is outside the scope of God's love, grace, and participation. And in all that we do we are encouraged to find ways to acknowledge that God is the One whom we love and serve.

Chapels, yes! But also godly practices in every dimension of the organization or business for which we are responsible. Christ is honored by worship but also by ethics, by prayer but also by generosity, by meditation but also by service.

Thought: Can we so live, speak, love, and serve that others will meet the Master?

Correction

The Wound That Heals

Better is open rebuke than hidden love. Wounds from a friend can be trusted.

PROVERBS 27:5-6

One of the great myths of the contemporary world is the notion of the autonomous human being. This person has need of no one. This person is accountable to no one.

Linked to the idea of the autonomous person are all sorts of ideas about self-sufficiency and freedom. And these ideas are very much the product of the Western world since the Enlightenment.

But there is also another vision of what it means to be a human being. This vision speaks of humans made in the image of God. It speaks of humans in relationship. It upholds the idea of covenant and of accountability.

The deepening of this vision speaks of our need of redemption and healing and of our calling to be part of the community of faith. This vision speaks of journeying together, of companionship, of Christ, and of care.

This vision speaks of spiritual friendships which both affirm and challenge us in the journey of faith; friendships which both consolidate and transform our spiritual journey.

This happy enterprise also involves the difficult art of correction. Mother Teresa observes, "Correction at times hurts most when it is most true."[145]

While we tend to see correction in negative terms, it is something quite different. Correction is an expression of love. And it is undoubtedly love's most difficult work. While love wishes it could be positive and affirming, love also has to be willing to do the hard work of calling us to greater fidelity, integrity, and wholeness.

This is the work of love that wounds in order to heal.

Reflection: In what ways do I need to be more open for the hard work of love to be done in my life?

Trust

Relying on the God of All Grace

> *I want to know Christ and the power of his resur-*
> *rection and the fellowship of sharing in his*
> *sufferings, becoming like him in his death.*
> PHILIPPIANS 3:10

There is no doubt about Mother Teresa's commitment to Jesus Christ. She states, "One thing
Jesus asks of me: that I lean on Him; that in Him
and only in Him I put complete trust; that I surrender myself to Him unreservedly."[146]

This is a powerful confession of trust and surrender. And it highlights one of the most central
impulses of Christian spirituality, namely, the
desire and faith to be in Christ and to partake in
his purposes. Saint Paul had a similar desire. And
we too can live in the desire to know Christ, to
trust him, and to live for him.

There is something wonderful and blessed
about living this way. There is also something pro-
foundly challenging about this way of life. To trust
Christ and to surrender to him mean that we are
no longer the center of the universe. It also

means that we now live to know and to please God. And furthermore it means that we may well have to walk the difficult road of relinquishment and suffering.

To know Christ is not only to know him in his power and blessedness. It also means that we know him in his abandonment and suffering. And this is where trust becomes such a key note. It is one thing to trust the God who blesses. It is another thing to trust the God who withholds or chastises us. It is one thing to live in the grace of Christ's resurrection. It is quite another to live in the grace of the Garden of Gethsemane.

To truly trust is to trust all that God gives us — joy and hardship; blessedness and relinquishment; and grace and suffering.

Reflection: Surrender and trust belong together. I trust the God to whom I surrender. And I trust all of his ways with me — the easy as well as the difficult.

Being a Blessing

Carriers of God's Grace and Love

Do not be overcome by evil, but overcome evil with good.

ROMANS 12:21

A central impulse to living the Christian life is that we seek to do good to others. We want to help not hinder, bless not curse, build up not tear down, encourage not alienate.

Mother Teresa also sees this as important. She advises, "Let no one ever come to you without coming away better and happier."[147]

But this desire to be a blessing to others must come from a good place. It can't come from guilt or self-aggrandizement. And it can't come from the need to be needed or from the desire to please others. Helping and serving people with these motivations and intentions won't in the long run bless others and certainly won't be good for us. Being a blessing must come from a very different place.

So where must this come from? It can only come from what we have received from Christ and from what Christ by the Spirit is seeking to do.

Being a blessing is not the attempt to be something special, nor is it the attempt to do something extraordinary. It has to do with being ourselves and being open to the Holy Spirit. Being a blessing is God breaking into the situation. It is God at work and our cooperation with the movement of God.

Thus being a blessing to others is being a channel of God's goodness and grace. And in this, people are drawn to God and not to us. God is glorified rather than that people make much of us.

To live this way is a big challenge for us. We can so easily be self-focused and preoccupied. But God calls us also to be aware of others and to do them good.

> *Prayer: Lord, help me to respond to what you want me to do for others, rather than for me to try to do what others may want.*
> *Amen.*

Giving

Sharing Beyond What Is Convenient

For even the Son of Man did not come to be served, but to serve, and to give his life as a ransom for many.

MARK 10:45

There are many ways in which we give. Sometimes we give with joy and great generosity. Most often we give without much thought. And sometimes we give grudgingly as if we are forced to do something against our will.

Mother Teresa has much to say about giving, but her central idea is that giving should be costly. Giving from our leftovers or from our abundance is not true giving. She challenges us to "Give to a point that it is difficult for you."[148]

But why this kind of giving? one may well ask. The answer to this lies close at hand—because it is the heart of the gospel.

God's self-giving is demonstrated in the gift of his Son, finally handed over into the cruel hands of sinful humanity. Jesus' self-giving is the gift of the Suffering Servant. He gives his life for the redemption of the world.

The Holy Spirit is the One poured out on the followers of Jesus. The Spirit brings gifts and graces. The Spirit's work is also all about self-giving.

If this is true of Father, Son, and Holy Spirit, it can hardly be less true of us who are called into the fellowship of the Trinity. We become small repetitions of who God is and the way God has manifested himself.

If the nature of God is to give, then we who share in God's life through Christ are also called to give. And what we are invited to give is not our surplus but our very selves in the service of God. Giving is self-giving. And this kind of giving is always costly. For in giving ourselves we embrace a small dying and a very real relinquishment.

This kind of giving spells grace for the other and transformation for ourselves. As such, we will gain what in other ways we would never be able to gain.

Reflection: Giving opens us to mysterious graces because it brings us in touch with the heart of God.

Holiness

Living in God's Transforming Presence

Then one of the seraphs flew to me with a live coal in his hand, which he had taken with tongs from the altar. With it he touched my mouth and said, "See, this has touched your lips; your guilt is taken away and your sin is atoned for."

ISAIAH 6:6-7

The Christian life is growth in love, holiness, and service. Holiness is growing in Godlikeness and this is the product of the grace of God and the empowerment of the Spirit. It is not the result of spiritual techniques.

Mother Teresa goes to the heart of the subject. She comments, "Nothing can make me holy except the presence of God."[149]

Living in God's presence is living in the light of God's Word and in the joy of the Spirit. It is living in prayer and solitude. It is living in listening to Scripture and in serving the neighbor.

Being in God's presence is not restricted to traditional religious activities. God has promised to accompany us in all of life. At home or at work I may experience God's grace and presence.

God's presence is a comforting, enlightening, and purifying presence. God sustains us. God guides us. And God makes us whole.

When we experience God as friend and companion, we become more like him. God's presence is a shaping and transforming presence and this is to make us more Christlike.

Christlikeness is the formation into the love and grace of Christ. It is becoming like Christ in obedience to God and in service to the neighbor. It is the growth to becoming a reconciling and healing presence in the many relationships of life.

Meditation: The secret of the Christian life is responding to what God wants to do in my life.

A Life of Faith

The Motivational Center
of the Christian Life

*This righteousness from God comes through faith
in Jesus Christ to all who believe.*

ROMANS 3:22

The center of the Christian life is not what we do. And it certainly is not our doing something to gain credit with God.

The story is wonderfully different. It is all about what God has done in Christ. It is about the free offer of new life as God's generous gift to us.

In faith we accept God's salvation. And in faith we live the whole of the Christian life in trust and obedience to the God who has made us whole.

Mother Teresa is equally sure about the centrality of faith even though she focuses on the relationship between faith and action. She notes, "Faith in action through prayer, faith in action through service: each is the same thing, the same love, the same compassion."[150]

A life of faith is never only directed toward God, although God is the center. And as the center, God is the One to whom we constantly look to in faith and trust. But the life of faith is also directed toward those with whom we are in relationship. In faith we pray for and serve our family members and those in the community of faith. We are also called to love and serve the neighbor, the stranger, and even the enemy.

Thus faith has a practical outworking. In faith we see the way in which we can bless and help the other. In faith we pray. In faith we serve.

Moreover, in faith we can see the other whole. And so we pray for God's empowering and transformative Spirit to be present and active, and we work so as to participate in what God is doing.

In faith we can see the rough places made smooth, the places of darkness made light, the barren places made fruitful, and the wounded places in our lives and world made whole.

Prayer: Lord, may I ever live in faith and trust in you, and may you give me the gift of faith to cast mountains into the sea. Amen.

Final Safekeeping

Into Thy Hands I Commit My Life

> *For I am already being poured out like a drink*
> *offering, and the time has come for my departure.*
> *I have fought the good fight, I have finished the*
> *race, I have kept the faith.*
>
> 2 TIMOTHY 4:6-7

On the fifth of September, 1997, Mother Teresa died. Her last words, as was her whole life, were marked by simplicity: "Jesus, I trust you."[151]

Mother Teresa was able to trust Jesus in her death with her safekeeping until the final resurrection in God's final future. This trust in the face of death had been forged and shaped by her trust in Jesus in the midst of life.

She had given herself in faith and trust to the service of God as a teaching nun. She had in faith responded to a second call to leave the order and start a new work among the poorest of the poor. And throughout the many following decades she had trusted Jesus that he would send her coworkers and bless this work. Trusting Jesus is both a gift of faith given by the Spirit and a posture of life that is forged in the midst of the joys, challenges, and hardships. Trust does not happen overnight. It is forged over the long haul as one experiences the Other as fully trustworthy.

This has been Mother Teresa's experience. It can also be ours. We, too, can trust in Jesus and experientially know him to be fully trustworthy. To know this great joy means that we must fully give ourselves to him in a life of faith, obedience, and service. In the challenges of life we find Jesus trustworthy. In our deepest need we find him trustworthy. In the difficulties of service we find him trustworthy.

And so in the time of our greatest need, in the hour of death, we too can say, "Jesus, I trust you."

Reflection: In life and in death our prayer
can be: Lord, into your hands
I commit my spirit.

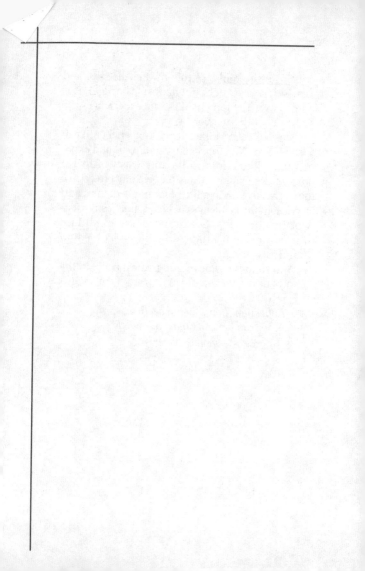

Appendix

A Brief Chronology of Mother Teresa

1910   Mother Teresa was born on August 16 as Agnes Gonxha Bojaxhiu in Skopje, the capital of the Albanian republic of Macedonia. She was the third and last child of Nikolle Bojaxhiu and Drana Bernai.

1910   On August 27, Agnes was baptized in the parish church of the Sacred Heart of Jesus. Her parents were Roman Catholic. And her mother, Drana, was a very devout woman.

1915-24 The early years of family life and schooling were happy ones for Agnes. The family was close-knit and spent almost as much time at church as they did at home. From a young age Agnes was interested in the lives of the saints and missionaries.

1919   Tragedy struck the family due to the death of Agnes' father. He was involved in municipal politics and may have died due to poisoning by some of his enemies.

1928	Agnes applies for admission to the Order of the Sisters of Our Lady of Loreto and does her initial training in Dublin.
1929	Arrives in Calcutta in early January and is sent to Darjeeling in the foothills of the Himalayas to begin her novitiate.
1931	On May 24 Agnes professes her temporary vows. She chose the name Teresa in honor of Teresa of the Little Flower (Therese of Lisieux).
1931-37	Sister Teresa serves in Calcutta as a geography and history teacher at St. Mary's School run by the Loreto Sisters.
1937	On May 24 she professes her final vows. She becomes director of studies at St. Mary's.
1946	September 10 was the great turning point in Sister Teresa's life. On a train from Calcutta to Darjeeling she receives a call within her call to serve the poor by living among them.
1948	On August 16, from her order and from Rome she receives permission to live as a religious (nun) outside of the

convent. She takes a three-month course in basic nursing and adopts a white sari like the ones worn by poor Indian women. The blue border symbolizes the desire to imitate the Virgin Mary. She is also granted, in this year, Indian citizenship.

1949   On March 19 Mother Teresa is joined by her first follower, a former student from St. Mary's School.

1950   On July 10 the Order of Missionaries of Charity is authorized by Rome. More former students join her.

1952   *Nirmal Hriday* (Home of the Pure Heart) is opened in Kalighat, a Hindu Temple in the heart of Calcutta. The home is for the destitute and dying.

1953   The Mother House of the Missionaries of Charity is founded and located at 54 Lower Circular Road in Calcutta. Later a house for slum children is opened and the sisters begin mobile clinics for lepers.

1962   Mother Teresa is honored by the Indian government with the Padma Sri Award (Order of the Lotus) and by

SEATO nations with the Magsaysay Award.

1965   On February 1 Pope Paul VI gives the Missionaries of Charity validity to be an order for the international Catholic Church.

1965-71 The order has grown to three hundred sisters. New homes for the poor and needy are opened in Venezuela, Africa, Australia, and Europe. By 1971 there are fifty homes in many parts of the world.

1969   The Co-Workers of the Missionaries of Charity—an international organiza-tion of supporting laypersons—is officially established on March 26.

1970s   Mother Teresa becomes more interna-tionally known through the work of Malcolm Muggeridge. She is awarded many prizes during this time: the Good Samaritan Award in the USA, the Templeton Award for Progress in Religion in the UK, and the Pope John XXIII Peace Prize.

1979   Mother Teresa is awarded the Nobel Peace Prize.

1980-85 The Missionaries of Charity continue to expand and many join the order. Homes now operate in Lebanon, Yugoslavia, Mexico, Brazil, Peru, Kenya, Haiti, Spain, Ethiopia, Belgium, and New Guinea. In one year, 1983, fourteen new homes are opened.

1986-89 The Missionaries of Charity are able to enter previously closed countries such as Ethiopia, Southern Yemen, Cuba, and Russia.

1986 Pope John Paul II visits Mother Teresa and her work in Calcutta.

1988-89 Mother Teresa is twice hospitalized due to heart trouble.

1990 On April 16, Mother Teresa steps down as the Superior General of her order due to ill health. In September she is re-elected to this position.

1991 Mother Teresa appeals to Presidents George Bush and Saddam Hussein to avert the Gulf War.

1991-93 Her health declines, and in this period she collapses while in Mexico and then again in Delhi, India.

1996   Mother Teresa is admitted to the hospital with a broken collarbone and later in that year is hospitalized with malarial fever. In October of this year she is made an honorary USA citizen.

1997   Sister Nirmala is elected as Mother Teresa's successor in March, and in September Mother Teresa passes away due to a heart attack.

Endnotes

1. Mother Teresa, 1986, p. 23.
2. Mother Teresa, 1988, pp. 44-45.
3. Mother Teresa, 1991, p. 61.
4. Mother Teresa, 1986, p. 39.
5. Zambonini, F., 1993, p. xi.
6. Muggeridge, M., 1972, p. 85.
7. Mother Teresa, 1995, p. 38.
8. Mother Teresa, 1999, p. 79.
9. Mother Teresa, 1986, p. 49.
10. Zambonini, F., 1993, p. 121.
11. Mother Teresa, 1995, p. 181.
12. Muggeridge, M., 1972, p. 54.
13. Mother Teresa, 1999, p. 71.
14. Mother Teresa, 1986, pp. 50-51.
15. Mother Teresa, 1986, p. 6.
16. Mother Teresa, 1995, p. 181.
17. Muggeridge, M., 1972, p. 65.
18. Mother Teresa, 1988, p. 64.
19. Mother Teresa, 1987, p. 133.
20. Mother Teresa, 1986, p. 100.
21. Mother Teresa, 1995, p. 115.
22. Zambonini, F., 1993, p. 75.
23. Muggeridge, M., 1972, p. 67.
24. Mother Teresa, 1987, p. 135.
25. Mother Teresa, 1988, p. 53.
26. Mother Teresa, 1987, p. 43.
27. Porter, D., 1986, p. 47.
28. Mother Teresa, 1987, p. 138.

29. Muggeridge, M., 1972, p. 67.
30. Mother Teresa, 1986, p. 68.
31. Zambonini, F., 1993, p. 72.
32. Mother Teresa, 1988, p. 52.
33. Mother Teresa, 1995, p. 140.
34. Porter, D., 1986, p. 25.
35. Muggeridge, M., 1972, p. 65.
36. Mother Teresa, 1995, p. 115.
37. Porter, D., 1986, p. 97.
38. Mother Teresa, 1985, p. 46.
39. Mother Teresa, 1995, p. 68.
40. Muggeridge, M., 1972, p. 39.
41. Mother Teresa, 1985, p. 51.
42. Mother Teresa, 1996a, p. 6.
43. Mother Teresa, 1996, p. 77.
44. Zambonini, F., 1993, p. 101.
45. Mother Teresa, 1996a, p. 16.
46. Mother Teresa, 1988, p. 72.
47. Mother Teresa, 1991, p. 83.
48. Mother Teresa, 1995, p. 42.
49. Doig, D., 1976, p. 97.
50. Mother Teresa, 1996, p. 122.
51. Mother Teresa, 1995, p. 56.
52. Zambonini, F., 1993, p.72.
53. Muggeridge, M., 1972, p. 87.
54. Mother Teresa, 1996, p. 71.
55. Mother Teresa, 1985, p. 53.
56. Mother Teresa, 1999, p. 81.
57. Mother Teresa, 1997, p. 66.
58. Mother Teresa, 1997a, p. 35.
59. Mother Teresa, 1988, p. 127.

60. Mother Teresa, 1996, p. 102.
61. Mother Teresa, 1995, p. 41.
62. Mother Teresa, 1985, p. 57.
63. Muggeridge, M., 1972, p. 75.
64. Mother Teresa, 1996, p. 25.
65. Mother Teresa, 1999, p. 162.
66. Mother Teresa, 1997a, p. 3.
67. Zambonini, F., 1993, p. 76.
68. Mother Teresa, 1995, p. 53.
69. Mother Teresa, 1987, p. 46.
70. Mother Teresa, 2002, p. 13.
71. Mother Teresa, 1993, p. 71.
72. Mother Teresa, 1985, p. 48.
73. Muggeridge, M., 1972, p. 98.
74. Mother Teresa, 1999, p. 159.
75. Mother Teresa, 1987, p. 46.
76. Mother Teresa, 1996, p. 64.
77. Mother Teresa, 1997, p. 35.
78. Mother Teresa, 1997a, p. 99.
79. Mother Teresa, 1999, p. 78.
80. Zambonini, F., 1993, p. x.
81. Mother Teresa, 2002, p. 137.
82. Mother Teresa, 1997, p. 103.
83. Mother Teresa, 1995, p. 56.
84. Mother Teresa, 1997a, p. 100.
85. Mother Teresa, 1997, p. 60.
86. Mother Teresa, 1987, p. 74.
87. Mother Teresa, 1991, p. 59.
88. Muggeridge, M., 1972, p. 112.
89. Mother Teresa, 1981, p. 38.
90. McGovern, J., 1978, p. 12.

91. Mother Teresa, 1997, p. 57.
92. Mother Teresa, 2002, p. 7.
93. Mother Teresa, 1985a, p. 1.
94. Mother Teresa, 1997a, p. 39.
95. Mother Teresa, 1999, p. 108.
96. Mother Teresa, 1985, p. 49.
97. Mother Teresa, 1981, p. 21.
98. Mother Teresa, 1987, p. 93.
99. Zambonini, F., 1993, p. 171.
100. Mother Teresa, 1986, p. 18.
101. Mother Teresa, 1997, p. 22.
102. Mother Teresa, 1995, p. 56.
103. McGovern, J., 1978, p. 8.
104. Mother Teresa, 1991, p. 71.
105. Le Joly, E., 1998, p. 102.
106. Mother Teresa, 2002, p. 151.
107. Mother Teresa, 1999, p. 113.
108. Mother Teresa, 1995, p. 57.
109. Doig, D., 1976, p. 159.
110. McGovern, J., 1978, p. 85.
111. Mother Teresa, 1999, p. 131.
112. Mother Teresa, 2002, p. 117.
113. Muggeridge, M., 1972, p. 69.
114. McGovern, J., 1978, p. 37.
115. Porter, D., 1986, p. 40.
116. Le Joly, E., 1998, p. 151.
117. Mother Teresa, 1995, p. 115.
118. Mother Teresa, 1997a, p. 34.
119. Mother Teresa, 1997, p. 47.
120. Mother Teresa, 1999, p. 69.
121. Muggeridge, M., 1972, p. 72.

122. Mother Teresa, 1985, p. 36.
123. Mother Teresa, 1986, p. 31.
124. Mother Teresa, 1988, p. 6.
125. Le Joly, E., 1998, p. 160.
126. Mother Teresa, 1995, p. 62.
127. Mother Teresa, 1993, p. 99.
128. Mother Teresa, 1999, p. 64.
129. Muggeridge, M., 1972, p. 66.
130. Mother Teresa, 2002, p. 164.
131. Mother Teresa, 1997a, p. 44.
132. Mother Teresa, 1995, p. 115.
133. Porter, D., 1986, p. 56.
134. Mother Teresa, 2002, p. 150.
135. Mother Teresa, 1995, p. 57.
136. Mother Teresa, 1999, p. 111.
137. Maalouf, J., 2000, p. 33.
138. Le Joly, E., 1998, p. 138.
139. Mother Teresa, 1988, p. 64.
140. Mother Teresa, 1987, p. 69.
141. Zambonini, F., 1993, p. 144.
142. Mother Teresa, 1999, p. 99.
143. Mother Teresa, 1985, p. 54.
144. Le Joly, E., 1998, pp. 12-13.
145. Mother Teresa, 1986, p. 123.
146. Mother Teresa, 2002, p. 85.
147. Mother Teresa, 1999, p. 172.
148. Mother Teresa, 1996, p. 83.
149. Mother Teresa, 1985, p. 55.
150. Mother Teresa, 1986, p. 66.
151. Le Joly, E., 1998, p. 197.

Bibliography

I Primary

Mother Teresa, 1981, *A Gift for God* (Compiled and introduced by Malcom Muggeridge), London: Fount.

Mother Teresa, 1985, *Mother Teresa: Contemplative in the Heart of the World* (Introduced by Brother Angelo Devananda Scolozzi), Ann Arbor: Servant Books.

Mother Teresa, 1985a, *My Life for the Poor* (Edited by Jose Luis Gonzalez-Balado and Janet N. Playfoot), San Franciso: Harper & Row.

Mother Teresa, 1986, *Jesus, the Word to be Spoken: Prayers and Meditations for Every Day of the Year* (Compiled by Brother Angelo Devananda Scolozzi), Ann Arbor: Servant Books.

Mother Teresa, 1987, *Heart of Joy* (Edited by Jose Luis Gonzalez-Balado), Ann Arbor: Servant Books.

Mother Teresa, 1988, *One Heart Full of Love* (Edited by Jose Luis Gonzalez-Balado), Ann Arbor: Servant Books.

Mother Teresa, 1991, *Loving Jesus* (Edited by Jose Luis Gonzalez-Balado), Ann Arbor: Servant Publications.

Mother Teresa, 1993, *The Best Gift Is Love: Meditations by Mother Teresa* (Compiled and edited by Sean-Patrick Lovett), Ann Arbor: Servant Publications.

Mother Teresa, 1995, *A Simple Path* (Compiled by Lucinda Vardey), New York: Random House.

Mother Teresa, 1996, *The Blessings of Love* (Selected and edited by Nancy Sabbag), Ann Arbor: Servant Publications.

Mother Teresa, 1996a, *Meditations from a Simple Path,* New York: Ballantine Books.

Mother Teresa, 1997, *In the Heart of the World: Thoughts, Stories & Prayers* (Ed. B. Benenante), Novato: New World Library.

Mother Teresa, 1997a, *In My Own Words* (Jose Luis Gonzalez-Balado), New York: Gramercy Books.

Mother Teresa, 1999, *Thirsting for God: A Yearbook of Prayers, Meditations and Anecdotes* (Compiled by Fr. Angelo Scolozzi), Ann Arbor: Servant Publications.

Mother Teresa, 2002, *No Greater Love*, Novato: New World Library.

II Secondary

Chawla, N., 1992, *Mother Teresa*, Rockport: Element Books.

Doig, D., 1976, *Mother Teresa: Her People and Her Work*, London: Collins.

Egan, E., 1985, *Such a Vision of the Street: Mother Teresa—The Spirit and the Work*, New York: Doubleday.

Hitchens, C., 1995, *The Missionary Position: Mother Teresa in Theory and Practice*, London: Verso.

Hobden, S. M., 1973, *Mother Teresa*, London: SCM.

Le Joly, E., 1983, *Mother Teresa of Calcutta: A Biography*, San Francisco: Harper & Row.

Le Joly, E., 1998, *We Do It For Jesus* (2nd Edition), Delhi: Oxford University Press.

Maalouf, J., 2000, *Praying with Mother Teresa*, Winona: Saint Mary's Press.

McGovern, J., 1978, *To Give the Love of Christ: A Portrait of Mother Teresa and the Missionaries of Charity*, New York: Paulist.

Mosteller, S., 1972, *My Brother, My Sister* (Inspired by Jean Vanier of L'Arche and Mother Teresa of Calcutta), Toronto: Griffin House.

Muggeridge, M., 1972, *Something Beautiful for God: Mother Teresa of Calcutta*, London: Collins.

Porter, D., 1986, *Mother Teresa: The Early Years*, Grand Rapids, Mich.: Eerdmans.

Sebba, A., 1997, *Mother Teresa: Beyond Image*, London: Weidenfeld & Nicolson.

Spink, K., 1997, *Mother Teresa: A Complete Authorized Biography,* San Francisco: Harper.

Zambonini, F., 1993, *Teresa of Calcutta: A Pencil in God's Hand,* New York: Alba House.

About the Author

Charles Ringma is an Australian trained at Reformed Theological College in Victoria. He holds degrees in divinity, sociology, and studies in religion. He has a Ph.D. in philosophical hermeneutics from the University of Queensland. He has served as a community worker among Aborigines as well as the poor in Manila, and has lectured at Asian Theological Seminary. He established Teen Challenge in Australia. He is presently professor of missions and evangelism at Regent College, Vancouver.

MORE INSPIRING AND CHALLENGING
MEDITATIONS FROM CHARLES RINGMA

Resist the Powers
Resist the Powers reveals an active faith that resists the powers of our age, embraces a vision of the kingdom of God, and brings head, heart, and hand together, combining spirituality with social transformation.　　1-57683-225-2

Dare to Journey
Written as a set of "conversations" with Henri Nouwen, these daily readings will transport you from a state of spiritual restlessness and seeking to retreat, renewal, re-evaluation, and prayer.　　1-57683-226-0

Seize the Day
This devotional by theologian and martyr Dietrich Bonhoeffer helps you see that it is possible to impact that world if you allow yourself to be transformed into the likeness of Christ.　　1-57683-216-3

Let My People Go
Captivating and inspirational, these 120 daily meditations challenge readers to remember the dream and legacy of Dr. Martin Luther King Jr.　　1-57683-423-9